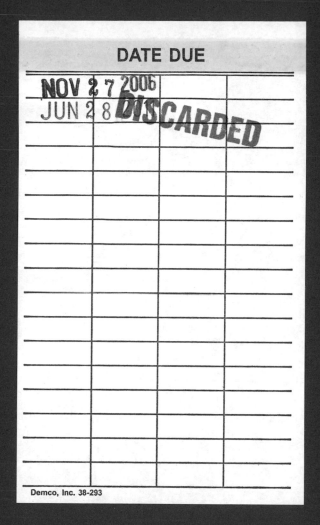

designing**borders**

First published in Great Britain in 2003 by Cassell Illustrated,
a division of Octopus Publishing Group Limited
2-4 Heron Quays, London E14 4JP

Distributed in the United States of America by
Sterling Publishing Co., Inc.,
387 Park Avenue South, New York, NY 10016-8810

A CIP catalogue record for this book is available from the British Library.

ISBN 1 844 03010 5

Printed in Hong Kong

designingborders

Noël Kingsbury

CASSELL
ILLUSTRATED

Contents

Rich colours combine at Hadspen
House in late summer: *Clematis
viticella* 'Viticella Rubra' covers
the kitchen garden wall behind
the tall stems of *Eupatorium
purpureum* 'Atropurpureum'
(rear left), cosmos hybrids
(front left) and *Cleome spinosa*
'Cherry Pink' (front right)

Introduction

Choosing and combining plants for borders is an art, a creative activity that for many people is the heart of gardening and the source of their passion for plants. Whereas lawns, hedges and vegetable patches are primarily functional, borders are about growing plants for the sheer enjoyment of gardening.

The 24 border plans created specially for this book show how today's leading professional designers use plants in different combinations, employing a wide range of styles for different situations. Some of the designs use plants as a means to an artistic end, while others are based on a love of the plants themselves. All take note, and this is a key point, of the conditions required by the plants.

Creating a beautiful border that will grow and change over time is, for many gardeners, a daunting prospect. The best way to start is by seeing how the experts do it, picking up tips and ideas, seeing how they arrange colours and leaf shapes, tall and small plants, and those with different textures. This book is an anthology of border schemes that show how successful and experienced designers use plants, and the kinds of plants they choose for particular situations. The plans demonstrate plant combinations for creating a particular effect, in a variety of styles and for different garden situations. Each is by a professional designer who is well known as a practising gardener.

John Brookes

is a prolific writer on garden design and is highly involved in the professional training of designers. He is associated with a contemporary approach to gardens, one that stresses the 'architecture' of plants chosen to fit his artistic vision.

Rupert Golby

is a busy practising garden designer whose approach is relatively traditional and plant orientated, showing sensitivity to surroundings and to his many clients.

Penelope Hobhouse

is known for her writings on colour scheming and garden history and for her association with high-profile garden designs and restorations. Her work involves meticulous research and a keen awareness of historical issues in gardening.

Noël Kingsbury

I am a writer and designer who advocates radical, ecologically based planting schemes. I have a passionate belief in the value of public space, for which nature-inspired plantings are often particularly effective.

Piet Oudolf

is a plantsman who brings a contemporary stance to the relationship between formality and lush planting. He runs a design practice and, with his wife Anja, a very successful nursery in Holland, specialising in grasses and perennials.

Nori and Sandra Pope

Today's colour gurus are a husband and wife team, who are gardeners and plantsmen rather than designers, and who have achieved recognition through the garden they have transformed and look after on a full-time basis at Hadspen House in Somerset, England.

[Left] Late season grasses and perennials are the high point of the year in Piet Oudolf's work: *Stipa calamagrostis, Achillea* 'Hella Glashof', *Astrantia* 'Ruby Wedding', *Monarda* 'Camanche' [rear right], *Persicaria amplexicaulis* 'Firedance' [front right]

[Right] At John Brookes' garden at Denmans, thistle-like *Eryngium giganteum* and other structural plants make for much visual stimulation

What was the brief?

The designers were asked to submit plans for four borders or plantings in a medium-sized garden. Beyond this there was no specification, though it was crucial that no one submitted anything too similar. The opportunity of designing a hypothetical scheme was meant to liberate the designers from the constraints within which they often have to work, helping them create designs that reflect their key interests and passions.

Such designs can sometimes be transferred direct from the page to a garden, but how often does that work? In established gardens there are many constraints or existing ingredients that have to be taken into account, ranging from the shape and style of the house and adjoining buildings, to features such as beautiful old trees that may be in the neighbouring garden. That is why it is dangerous to fall in love with a show garden at a horticultural exhibition, and imagine it can be installed without any modifications at home. By itself, it is fine, but how will it link up with the site?

Inspirational ideas, therefore, must be combined with practical needs. If a particular design in the book does inspire you, and actually fits a site in your own garden, it is imperative that you do some preliminary homework. First, make sure that its style blends, and does not jar, with the style of your surroundings. And second, check that the plants suit your garden's aspect, soil and climate by looking them up in a plant encyclopaedia (and if you can not provide their needs, find alternative plants that will be happy there). If, though, the plan is too large for your small garden, scale down and modify the design while making sure that you provide all-year interest using either evergreens or a seasonal succession of flowering plants. Alternatively, use one of these plans as a starting point for your own design, choosing your own colour scheme and plants with attractive shapes and textures.

The designers have submitted carefully thought out drawings as they might for a client. These designs are for medium-sized gardens with neutral soil and normal conditions, unless stipulated otherwise. An estimated number of plants required has also been supplied as a rough guideline.

The changing look of border styles

Before looking at the following designs, and examining the key criteria in creating a border, it helps if we have a quick look at how borders have developed over the years, giving the 24 designs a context.

There have been borders of some kind ever since people started growing plants for pleasure, but it was not until the late 19th century that they really began to acquire a life of their own. Complex shapes and patterns were developed, often incorporating displays of exotic and tender bedding plants. The early years of the 20th century saw an increasing interest in hardy plants rather than tender ones and, in Britain and central Europe especially, the border became a focus for herbaceous perennials. The herbaceous border reached its apogee in Edwardian England as a majestic spectacle (orchestrated by armies of gardeners), putting on its grand finale in late summer.

Since this high point early in the 20th century, the trend has been towards a more relaxed garden style. In England, Gertrude Jekyll created borders that played with sophisticated colour schemes; she often worked to architectural garden layouts designed in conjunction with her collaborator, the architect Edwin Lutyens. Later, the writer Vita Sackville-West brought a sense of cottage-like informality to her highly influential garden at Sissinghurst, in Kent, keeping her readers up to date of her progress in her newspaper articles.

Meanwhile, in central Europe, gardening was dominated more by perennials than shrubs. This was because many of the shrubs that are hardy in Britain or France were likely to be killed, or cut back to ground level, by their intensely cold winters. The leading figure in gardening with perennials and grasses at this time was the highly influential German garden designer (and possibly most influential of all time), Karl Foerster. A nurseryman and prolific writer, in the 1930s and 1950s he began to promote a naturalistic style using grasses and natural species perennials. While Foerster's work has been little recognized in Britain, his legacy has been immensely important in central Europe and the USA. Wolfgang Oehme, of the American Oehme Van Sweden design partnership, was trained in the Foerster tradition, while Piet Oudolf also regards him as a major contemporary influence. (This influence is discussed on page 150.)

If there has been an 'end result' over the last century of innovation and experimentation, it has been the mixed border. Since few amateur gardeners have ever had the space for borders devoted entirely to perennials or summer annuals, there has always been a tendency to combine these different plants within one border. The mixed border therefore fulfils a variety of different functions: the shrubs provide spring flowers, structure and screening; bulbs create spring displays; perennials bring

summer and autumn colour; and annuals make an appearance in odd gaps for extra summer interest.

Recent developments have seen a much greater use of climbers in borders, clambering up supports such as obelisks, wigwams of canes and other purpose-built structures, and the introduction of vegetables, exploiting the intense colours of, for example, ruby chard, red cabbage and red lettuce. And while the archetypal borders of the Edwardian era were very neat, with a careful gradient from the tallest plants at the back to the shortest at the front, there has since been a tendency towards a more informal structuring of heights. The apparently artless jumble of the cottage garden style has been a considerable influence in this respect. Yet planting styles still heavily relied on a backdrop – a hedge, wall or fence – which meant that the plants could be seen from a limited range of viewpoints.

A major breakthrough came in the 1960s with the popularization of 'island beds' by nurseryman Alan Bloom. Surrounded by oceans of lawn, they incorporated shrubs and perennials, usually built around a 'hill' of taller plants in the centre. The island beds injected greater flexibility into mixed borders by allowing plant combinations to be appreciated from a variety of angles. Beth Chatto's garden, in Essex, in the UK, also became highly influential from this time on, with its informal, fluid layout, and plants usually chosen to match the prevailing conditions.

The most recent changes to the border have come from an awareness of how plants grow in nature, often in distinct groups. German public landscapes, with their marked, naturalistic style, have been a particular focus of interest. These plantings lie somewhere between a conventional herbaceous border and a wildflower meadow. They are open, with narrow paths winding through perennials and ornamental grasses arranged in romantic drifts. Dutch designers, such as Mien Ruys and Piet Oudolf, have also made us look at border plants in different ways, the former within a strongly architectural framework, the latter through the evocation of a more romantic style, concentrating on the use of plant shape and form.

Preliminary practicalities

What do I want from my border?

It is vital that you clarify the purpose of your border. Is it meant to be a showpiece, or somewhere to grow favourite plants? Should it double as a boundary, running beside a fence or hedge for example, or be placed in a lawn? And will it include tall plants so that it is looked up at, or low ones so that it is looked over?

Next, consider the immediate surroundings. The new border can be used to fill a gap or bare space, for example a right-angled corner between two walls, or to cover a bank or hide an eyesore. John Brookes' designs are particularly helpful when it comes to arranging plants right in front of a building, and often include strongly structural plants to complement their surroundings. Sunny, sheltering, backdrop walls also mean that some borders can incorporate sub-tropical plants, because they like the extra heat and protection (see my and Penelope Hobhouse's designs on pages 134–137 and 110–113). By clarifying the purpose of the border, it becomes clear which type of plants you need.

Positioning borders

The dimensions of your garden determine the maximum size of the border, and there is nothing you can do about that, but you can decide where you put it.

First and foremost, a border needs to be positioned where it can be seen, either from the house or a seating area in the garden. In fact, borders are often designed in conjunction with a seating area or a feature, such as a barbecue. Conventionally, it has been assumed that we need to stand back from a border in order to see it, but recent designs have challenged this approach. They have also blurred the boundaries, in gravel gardens, between the paths and border planting (see Rupert Golby's blue and yellow border and the Pope's dry gravel bed on pages 86–89 and 180–183).

Another development has seen the use of narrow paths through dense planting to offer a more intimate view of the scheme. Such paths are an important feature of contemporary German plantings (see my design on pages 130–133) and, to an extent, of Piet Oudolf's work. In fact, one recent development lets people look down over the planting from raised decking, while planting on banks means you can also look up at the plants (see my design on pages 122–125).

Border backdrops

Borders have traditionally had a backdrop, such as a wall or fence, but this can be very limiting, allowing plants to be looked at only head-on, 'like soldiers on parade', to quote the head of the leading German horticultural research institute. But deciding whether you need a backdrop depends on what you want to grow.

A traditional dark green yew hedge nicely shows off pastel flower colours, but you can get the same effect in an island bed with a distant view of a wall of conifers. Fresh green, blue and yellow flowers look effective against brick walls. Open borders or large island beds, with only a distant backdrop, suit the larger ornamental grasses best, and tall, robust perennials. And where there is no clear division with your neighbour's garden, a new border (even without a backdrop) helps provide privacy and define the end of your garden. Use climbers growing up sturdy trellis panels to enhance the effect.

A bank of poor soil is planted up with stress-tolerant plants in the author's own garden, including mauve *Lavandula stoechas* subsp. *pedunculata* and yellow *Euphorbia seguieriana* subsp. *niciciana*

The right conditions

While full sun supports the widest range of garden flora,
a wide variety of plants flourish in light, damp or heavy
shade (see John Brookes', Penelope Hobhouse's and my
designs on pages 58–61, 102–105 and 126–129). However,
unless you are drawn to the more subtle beauties of
woodland plants, aim for a site that gets as much sun
as possible.

Lighting

Sites that receive sun all year long offer more scope
for trouble-free gardening and design possibilities.
But thinking about how light hits the plants is crucial,
particularly in the winter when the sun is often at a low
angle. Piet Oudolf has done more than most modern
designers to draw our attention to how light affects the
way we see plants, particularly ornamental grasses
that often needing back-lighting to look their best.

Selecting the right plants for the right site

Soil conditions

The condition of the soil can cause a lot of heartache, especially to new gardeners. Much of this is due to a feeling that only one sort of soil is good for gardening, and that is the fine, crumbly tilth seen on TV garden programmes. But few of us have this, and if you do not it certainly is not a problem.

If you do have extremely good soil it means that you can grow the widest range of plants. Less perfect soils mean you must choose plants that enjoy the prevailing conditions. However, there are some situations that are difficult at the best of times, and they include heavy clay subsoil, extensive tree roots and soil that is full of rubble and rubbish. Where this is impossible to avoid, it will be necessary to improve the soil with large quantities of well-rotted organic matter, for example manure, agricultural waste (such as spent hops), and plant-derived compost, that should be dug in before planting and applied annually as a soil conditioner thereafter. Where soil conditions are very bad, try buying top quality topsoil and grow a border in a raised bed, so that the plants have about 30cm (1ft) of good soil to grow in.

There are two important criteria. The first is, will existing plants nearby have any impact? For example, if there are several large rhododendrons in the background, your choice of border flowers may create a colour clash. Make sure that the border plants look good in relation to each other, and to those nearby (see John Brookes' and my designs on pages 54–57 and 126–129).

The second point is that you must choose plants that will thrive in your border's soil and climate. Areas which often pose a problem to new gardeners include . . .

Hot dry sites, or soils that are light and free-draining

There is a wide selection of drought-resistant plants, most of which flower in spring and/or early summer. They often have attractive evergreen foliage, with popular Mediterranean flora recognizable by its low shrubby growth and grey leaves.

Try a border based on lavender, sage, thyme and rock roses, with the use of gravel. Gravel is a good mulch, reducing evaporation from the soil in dry spells, and is ideal in dry gardens (see John Brookes' contemporary border, Rupert Golby's scented border and the Popes' gravel garden, on pages 62–65, 78–81 and 180–183).

Wet soil

Moist soil can be a boon, allowing many lush-growing plants to flourish, but if water sits in pools when it rains or there is regular flooding, only those species that originate from wetlands will survive. The rest will rot and die.

Wet environments encourage the growth of luxuriant vegetation with lots of tall, rapidly-growing stems, usually with flowers in the latter part of the year like, for example, the big yellow ligularias. A border on such wet soil will probably feature several shrubs tolerant of occasional flooding (willows) and large perennials, many of which have striking foliage and are very colourful in late summer, for example species of sanguisborba and eupatoriums. The Popes are particularly skilful in combining dramatic colours and shapes – even in damp conditions (see their damp border on pages 176–179).

Shade

Few plants from open, sunny habitats will grow satisfactorily in shade, and if they do make good growth they might not flower. There are, however, a large number of plants from woodland habitats that will flourish in shade, especially if it is not very deep or the soil is not dry for long periods. Most are spring flowering, but many have attractive leaves that look good all summer and, since many are evergreen, there is no reason why a shady area should not look good all year. Most flowering woodland plants are low-growing bulbs and perennials, but there are some taller foliage plants, such as bamboos and a few shade-tolerant flowering shrubs, for example species of ribes, sarcococca or, for deep shade, *Danae racemosa*.

A shady border will probably be on the low side but with an interesting variation of foliage colour, shape and texture. (Penelope Hobhouse's design for a north-facing border, on pages 102–103, is a good starting point. Mine, pages 126–129, shows how planting can reflect the gradient from deep to light shade.)

The garden at the Old
Rectory, Sudborough,
designed by Rupert
Golby, features a large
natural pond where
damp-loving plants thrive

Exposed sites

Wind will damage many plants, making it impossible to
grow some common border varieties either because of
physical damage (with tall plants being blown over) or
because of the desiccation of delicate leaves. Since cold
winds are particularly damaging, restrict your plants to
those that are reliably hardy. Though this rules out tall
perennials, many smaller ones can be used, as can many
shrubs, plants with tiny leaves (heathers) and ornamental
grasses (*Molinia caerulea*) that simply and beautifully
bend in the wind.

Coastal sites

Plants will need to be salt- and wind-tolerant to grow on
the coast. Those with silver or grey foliage are often a good
choice because the coating of tiny hairs, which provide the
distinct colour, is a protective device against desiccation
and the salt particles blown in from the sea. When
selecting a colour scheme, grey foliage is an obvious
starting point, in conjunction with purple or bronze leaves
or pastel-coloured flowers.

Coastal gardens do have one big advantage though,
because the sea moderates cold winter temperatures.
This provides a good environment for frost tender, wind-
tolerant evergreens, such as hebes and olearias. They
could be the basis of a planting scheme, their attractive
evergreen foliage making a wonderful combination
with other plants, such as many ornamental grasses.
(Penelope Hobhouse's mixed shrub border in full sun,
pages 106–109, is a possibility for such a scheme.
My steppe planting, pages 122–125, is also suitable for
coastal or exposed locations.)

The aesthetics

Which style?

The environment of the site might suggest a starting point for your design, while other elements may provide an inspiration. An old country house, for example, may suggest a cottage garden border, a finely proportioned house might demand something more formal, while a modern house or surroundings suggest a border with many ornamental grasses and other simple, elegant forms. The fine sense of balance created by Penelope Hobhouse's 'repeating plants' (see pages 98–101) and the occasional symmetrical planting in Rupert Golby's designs (pages 74–81) work well in the vicinity of older houses. With contemporary architecture, try the more modernist asymmetry of John Brookes' designs (pages 50–65) which are particularly successful at softening areas dominated by brick and concrete.

You can also opt for a wide range of other choices, such as a Mediterranean-style border, a border based on a particular group of plants (roses), or plants with a similar look (architectural plants), or plants that are richly scented. The final consideration is, do you want the border at its best at particular times (spring, midsummer and early autumn) or staying attractive right through the year? (Rupert Golby is particularly skilled at building plant combinations that always look attractive; see his year-round border on pages 74–77.)

Colour

Most people want to explore the possibilities of a particular colour or combination of colours. This theme can be continued through as much of the year as possible, or just for one season. (Penelope Hobhouse's designs on pages 98–113 have a strong sense of colour harmony, and are well worth studying.)

One-colour borders

They are relatively easy and fun to make, and can look very sophisticated. The Popes have dedicated much of their gardening to exploring the possibilities of monocolour planting, believing that the result creates a strong sense of harmony. Having a single colour also makes people seek out the subtle differences between each plant, in terms of tone and shape.

White has good possibilities for long-term interest, and is delightfully cool. Yellow is a good spring to early autumn possibility, but can have limitations if too many hard golden yellows are used. Blue/mauve is interesting to use because the tones vary significantly, though the number of true blues is limited. And red can be tricky choice, at least until late summer, because there is not a vast amount of choice before then. It is also quite a dark colour en masse, creating a surprisingly sombre effect.

Two-colour borders

Two colour borders involve a bit more skill but also create an image of sophistication. The key to understanding how two-colour borders work is the colour wheel. Colours that are next to each other, such as pink and blue, and yellow and green, are harmonious combinations. Those opposite each other are more startling combinations, such as yellow and blue, orange and purple, and scarlet and green. They can be very striking but are not to everyone's taste.

The blue and yellow combination is quite easy to work with, partly because there are many plants to choose from in these colours, and partly because the colours 'spark off each other' without being strident. You can now also find a wide variety of plants with yellow foliage, for example the grassy *Carex elata* 'Aurea' and the popular tree *Robinia pseudoacacia* 'Frisia', both of which make an excellent background to blue or blue-violet flowers. (Also see Penelope Hobhouse's yellow and blue border backed by a yew hedge, on pages 110–113, which offers several flushes of these two colours through the growing season.)

Blue/violet and pink combinations are also easily created because there is a huge variety of suitable plants from which to choose. It is very much an early to midsummer combination, the classic 'olde English garden' look being shrub roses under-planted with blue/violet and pink geraniums, with nearby catmint and lavender. It may be a cliché, but it certainly is very restful. (The Popes have come up with novel plum and orange colour schemes on pages 170–183. You can easily adopt this idea choosing your own two-colour scheme.)

A red border at Hadspen House in mid-summer: the red of *Crocosmia* 'Lucifer' and *Achillea* 'Feuerland' is complemented by the dark foliage of *Prunus* × *cistena*

Pastel schemes

Pastel schemes using one or more colours can be extended to include bolder shades, such as the magenta *Geranium psilostemon* or purple-red *Knautia macedonica*, or even some of the remarkably deep-coloured dahlias now available. You can either let the strong colours dominate and add the lighter ones for relief, or alternatively use pastels with a few stronger highlights – it is entirely a matter of taste.

Hot schemes

Hot schemes are increasingly popular with their use of bright, jazzy colours. Red, orange and yellow are a popular combination, wonderful for summer and autumn. While there are plenty of yellows available, the number of oranges and good reds is more limited. Tropical climates tend to produce more oranges and reds, but these tender plants tend to flower late in the season though they certainly create quite a spectacle. Adding plants with purple or bronze foliage is also popular because they help to separate the strong colours without diminishing the overall effect.

And do not forget, whichever colour scheme you do choose, it can easily be changed at various times. For example, yellow and blue in spring (using daffodils and scillas) can be followed by pink and blue in early summer (from geraniums and lavenders) that, in turn, is replaced by yellow and blue in late summer (with rudbeckias and asters). The art of creating a good border is making sure there is a constant flow of colour. The best way to achieve this is to visit a garden centre every six weeks or so buying what is in flower. And learn how to avoid putting startling colours next to a feature plant which might detract attention from it. Also learn to use some plants as background fillers to help show off your favourites.

The all-season border

Many gardeners want something that always looks good in high profile positions, around the front door for example. But a good seasonal spread may mean that its virtues are spread thinly, so that it never looks spectacular. Evergreens will inevitably play a large part, and that can mean that the lack of seasonal change leads to boredom. The key is to have a wide variety of evergreens, perhaps using some coloured foliage, or to pay great attention to plant form and leaf shape and texture, such as mixing bamboos, ivies and hollies.

Along with the evergreens, include some perennials or deciduous shrubs that have good form, or interesting leaf shapes, which will provide spring to autumn interest. Finally aim to have some really worthwhile flowers that succeed each other. There probably won't be space for many combinations that flower altogether so think of one flowering plant for each month of the growing season and then consider some leaf/flower combinations that look good like a pink rose with a silver leaved artemesia.

The one-season border

In situations where it is not vital that everything always looks good all the time, it can be very rewarding to create borders that are spectacular for a couple of months with reduced interest for the rest of the year. An example might be a shaded area which can be made into a wonderfully colourful spring border but which is a more restrained collection of leaf shapes for the rest of the year. Another example would be a modern variant of the classical herbaceous border, a late summer to mid-autumn crescendo of colour and form, but with only a scattering of bulbs in spring and a few small perennials in early summer.

Those who love colour, will find this approach very satisfying, an opportunity to create exciting combinations of saturated colour. Those with space may be able to combine a backdrop of evergreens and a foreground of seasonal plantings or islands of short-interest colour amongst longer season plantings. Penelope Hobhouse is particularly good at doing this, as her first love, surprisingly as the author of *Colour in your Garden* (HarperCollins, 1985), is evergreen shrubs. The areas that the Popes plant at Hadspen are highly saturated with colours and tend to need high levels of maintenance to look good over a long season. Their gravel garden (pages 180–183) will last over a relatively long season, whereas their other plans will have a late season

Many shrubs, which
by nature have an
amorphous shape, can
be made to look
'architectural' with
some imaginative
pruning. In Penelope
Hobhouse's garden
such shrubs give
structure to the
otherwise relaxed,
informal planting

Height and shape

Plants need combining both for their colours and shapes so that they make a harmonious whole. A border entirely composed of low, hummocky shapes may be necessary on an exposed site, but will be rather dull. A few, dramatically vertical plants can make all the difference, for example the upright yew *Taxus baccata* 'Fastigiata'. (See John Brookes' plan for a small town garden, pages 54–57.) The opposite case, with too many upright growers, will conversely make it difficult to see what is happening behind the plants.

The traditional border has always put the tall plants at the back and the short ones at the front, with island beds having the tall ones in the centre. These principles do not need to be stuck to but it is important to ensure that you can see everything you are growing. For example, interlocking erect and ground-covering perennials provide interesting shapes and visual harmony.

Structure

Borders can be beautifully coloured and arranged but still look a mess. The reason is that there is not enough (or too much) structure. Borders without a few plants providing bold foliage, or composed entirely of plants with amorphous shapes, will be boring. Conversely a border with too many different shapes can be as fussy as one with too many colours.

Plants such as irises and grasses, with their linear leaves, are particularly useful for varying the pace of a border because they contrast with the leaf shapes of most border perennials and shrubs. More dramatic leaf shapes are provided by the likes of yuccas and phormiums (see John Brookes' contemporary border on pages 62–65). Bamboos, large grasses (miscanthus), upright conifers (cypresses), clipped box and yew are also good choices when it comes to injecting architectural shapes into a border.

Foliage

Strongly structural elements play a major role in nearly all the designs in this book. The exceptions are my naturalistic designs (see pages 122–137). Not that they are totally devoid of structure – the structure of ornamental grasses and perennials is just more subtle and seasonal than many of the large-leaved perennials (hostas) and evergreens (bamboos, hollies and phormiums). The strong element of repetition and mingling of varieties, is also an alternative to conventional structure in some naturalistic designs.

A strong development in recent years has been the greater focus given to form and foliage, with hardy exotic or tropical-looking plants becoming very fashionable. Well-sited they can be very dramatic, but they are also in danger of becoming a cliché (or oddity) if they are used where the visually attention-seeking foliage is out of place, for example in rural areas. But in the right place, certainly a sheltered one, it is possible to have a lot of fun with exotica. (In my exotic garden, on pages 134–137, I deliberately go over the top in using these plants.)

Foliage lasts a lot longer than flowers and has more potential than gardeners often realize. Coloured foliage plants have always been popular and a scattering of silver variegation or yellow- or purple-tinged leaves can transform a border over a long season. Such colours can also be used to complement flower colours with, for example, cream variegation looking beautifully cool with white flowers, while gold or yellow complements blue or violet, and purple leaves look stunning with orange or yellow. Light coloured foliage is also a boon in the dark winter months.

Beware, though, of using too many different foliage tints and patterns in one border. To many eyes, gold and silver do not mix, while putting variegated patterns together can look terribly fussy. The keynote is restraint.

The plant categories

Shrubs

Shrubs are bulky and take up space, dividing the border into smaller portions, controlling what can be seen while obscuring other plants. They are essential for height and shape in the winter to early spring period, when most perennials are still underground. The main criticisms are that most shrubs flower early, and far too many look dull for the rest of the year. Also, many have amorphous, uninteresting shapes which make those that do have a distinct form, such as the layered branches of *Viburnum plicatum* 'Mariesii', such valuable garden plants.

In fact, viburnums are some of the most useful spring-flowering shrubs, with roses being the most popular for summer. Rhododendrons and azaleas are really only for those who have acid soil but note that, like all dark evergreens, the former can be oppressive when not in flower.

Climbers

Vital for clothing backdrop walls and fences, climbers can also be allowed to scramble over shrubs. For example, let a small summer-flowering clematis clamber over a spring-flowering shrub, creating interest through two seasons. Climbers can also be grown on supports such as obelisks and wigwams.

Most climbers flower in early summer, but it is increasingly possible to find varieties that flower earlier or later, as the range sold by nurseries becomes more adventurous. Clematis are the largest group of climbers, with something for every taste and almost every season. Honeysuckles are also popular, as are roses, but the latter are often difficult to send in the required direction and do not offer the same coverage as do most climbers. And do not forget the foliage climbers, such as Virginia creeper (*Parthenocissus quinquefolia*) and vines that are attractive over a long season, often with spectacular autumn colours.

Perennials

Perennials are the mainstay of the border, with progressively more coming into flower through the year with the climax in late summer, and a tailing off until mid- or late autumn. The early flowering perennials, such as pulmonarias, geraniums and bergenias, tend to be low and hummocky, while the later ones often have a highly distinctive, upright form, such as asters, goldenrods and sunflowers.

One of the great advantages of perennials is that they quickly get established. It takes years for a shrub to show its full potential, but only a couple for a perennial. They also tend to be easy to propagate by division, providing extra plants for repeat planting which makes them very useful in naturalistic borders like mine, where much of the impact comes from the repetition of a relatively limited number of varieties.

Ornamental grasses

Garden grasses can be divided into two categories: those that are grown for their coloured foliage, such as carex and hakonechloa, and the larger ones that are used for their structural aspects, such as miscanthus and the popular *Stipa gigantea*. Many of the former are evergreen, making them very useful when creating long-season colour combinations and for cheering up exposed situations. The larger ones are marvellous for adding structure to borders, and for a sense of continuity, linking summer to winter, their flowers turning into seed heads that often look highly decorative until late winter. Piet Oudolf's designs use grasses to great effect.

Climbers, shrubs and perennials are used to create this stunning, shocking pink and green border at Hadspen house

[Left] In the yellow border at Hadspen House, the perennial fennel [*Foeniculum vulgare*] is grown through the pampas grass *Cortaderia selloana* 'Aureolineata'

[Right] Sweet peas run up arches over a path through the potager designed by Rupert Golby at the Old Rectory, Sudborough

Bulbs

Bulbs are vital for spring colour, and are generally remarkably easy to grow. Snowdrops, crocuses and daffodils are particularly reliable, forming clumps that increasingly get bigger each year. Bulbs are also easy to dot around other border plants, surrounding late emerging perennials and flowering in front of shrubs, particularly tulips, which in a cool climate have to be treated as an annual. Summer-flowering bulbs, such as lilies, and the autumn-flowering ones, such as colchicums and cyclamen, are equally useful, although it may be more difficult to find space for them amongst fuller later-season planting.

Annuals

Annuals and tender plants used for temporary summer effects, such as pelargoniums and marguerites, are often very colourful over a long summer season, making them essential components of the 'instant border'. A mixed border may well involve leaving spaces between shrubs and perennials so that there is room for different coloured annuals each summer. They can also be used to fill spaces between plants that take several years to reach their full size. Traditional hardy annuals, such as love-in-the-mist (*Nigella damascena*) and pot marigold (*Calendula officinalis*), can be sown directly into the ground.

Vegetables

Though slightly unconventional in the ornamental border, many herbs and vegetables make attractive plants and can be used in a similar way to annuals, filling spaces between perennials. The big disadvantage is that harvesting spoils the pattern. Even so, it is well worth using red lettuce and chicory, ruby-coloured perennial beet or chard, dark-leaved beetroot and purple-leaved basil. Those with attractive flowers, such as scarlet runner beans, can also play a part. (The Popes potager on pages 168–171 is an example of how effective coloured vegetables can be.)

Getting down to it: making and maintaining borders

Planning

Making a plan, even a crude one that is not to scale, will organize your thoughts. It is vital when calculating how many plants you need to buy if you are laying out the border all at once. Most good reference books and some garden centre labels indicate the eventual size of the plant, helping you work out the spacings. Note that it takes perennials two to three years to reach their full size, and shrubs even longer.

Perennials should be planted so that they just touch or slightly overlap after the first or second year, while shrubs should be spaced well apart leaving gaps between for perennials or annuals. Do not place the latter too close to the shrubs' woody growth; leave a gap of 40–50cm (16–20in).

Planning also enables you to work out how best to repeat plants, which is essential if the planting is to have any unity and coherence. A particularly good way of creating a successful border is to choose a theme plant for every one or two-month period through the spring and summer to which every other colour is related. Theme plants could include a large, dominating shrub or climber or, in the case of smaller perennials, a variety that is repeated by scattering several such plants across the border.

Soil preparation and weeding

Much fuss has been made about soil preparation before planting. This is because it was thought that any soil that fell short of a certain standard was deficient and had to be improved. But it is important to note that even quite difficult soils can be used as the starting point for attractive plantings, if the chosen plants actually like those soils. Clay is a good case. Because it is so hard to work, being lumpy and heavy, people tend to regard it as a real problem, but many shrubs actually flourish in it, roses especially, as do many perennials. Clay is a problem for those who need to cultivate the soil on a regular basis when growing vegetables and annuals, but for those making a permanent planting it is a once-only nuisance.

While our ideas on soil are changing, they are not when it comes to weeds. I cannot over-stress the importance of weeding, especially if you know that you have problem weeds, such as ground elder, creeping thistle or bindweed. They are very competitive plants which, if not eliminated, will create problems in the future. Chemical weed control is the best option. Despite claims to the contrary, there is very little evidence that modern herbicides, such as those containing the biodegradable ingredient glyphosate, present any appreciable danger to the environment and, in any case, such herbicides need only be used once.

Care and cultivation

For those who are organic, cover the ground with old carpet weighed down by stones or soil for one growing season and the weeds beneath will die, though some may come up through holes and around the edges. Dig them out, with every last bit of root.

Once the weeds have been eliminated, it is usually possible to start planting, but the soil does need to be moist. Often planting is made easier if the ground is cultivated first, perhaps with a rotovator to break up the soil. Unless this is very poor, there is little point in digging in manure or compost, or adding nutrients such as fertilizers. Most ornamental plants cannot utilize the levels of fertilizers often recommended for them, and the chemicals will only encourage the growth of weeds which use them more effectively.

Since woody plants are slow to establish it is worth making sure that you give them the right conditions. The soil well below the level of the rootball, and to its side, should be broken up to help aerate it, enabling water to drain away quickly and encourage the roots to spread. Care should be taken that the soil level mark on the trunk or stem remains the same as when in the pot.

It also helps, especially when the plants are pot-bound (ie the container is packed with roots that start poking out of the drainage holes), if you gently tease out the roots so that they grow in all directions and not round and round in a downward spiral, providing greater stability. It is now considered potentially harmful to add organic matter to a planting hole because it can encourage waterlogging. Soil returned to the planting hole should be well firmed in and watered to eliminate any air pockets.

Perennials, being much faster to establish, do not need such careful planting. Ideally, on heavy soil, the ground around the planting hole should be broken up if it has not already been done, the roots teased out of the rootball, with the soil then firmed down around them. In fact perennials can be planted with the minimum of care, even in less than ideal ground, provided they are firmly wedged into moist soil.

Getting established

Perhaps more crucial than the planting technique is the timing. In maritime-influenced climates with mild wet winters, the best time to plant is in the autumn or early winter because the plants will get established before there is any risk of summer drought. In regions with severe or prolonged winter cold, woody plants are best planted in the autumn, but perennials are liable to be frost-heaved out of the ground if put in then. Keep them in a cold frame until the spring. Areas with a continental climate tend to have only a very limited window of opportunity for perennial planting, and that is the period immediately after the worst of the winter.

The 'establishment phase' is the first year after planting for perennials, and a somewhat longer period for woody plants. If plants survive this, they will be better able to cope with subsequent difficult conditions or neglect.

All plants must be kept watered during their first year in periods of drought, even plants that are drought-resistant. Watering that is occasional but thorough will do far more good than frequent light watering, which often only wets the top of the soil, encouraging roots to stay there instead of delving downwards. Indeed, there is a point in delaying watering for as long as possible after planting to encourage them to do precisely this.

Weeding is also essential in the first year, otherwise your new plants will be up against stiff competition. Seedlings need to be hoed off, and larger plants hand-pulled or dug out. Weed and grass competition is the worst enemy of young trees and shrubs (as are adjacent, strongly growing ornamental perennials), and it is vitally important that you keep them away from the base of the plants for at least three years after planting.

Both weed competition and drying out can be greatly reduced by using a 3–5cm (1½–2in) deep wood chip mulch around the new plants. It suppresses the weeds and locks moisture in the ground. Take care not to allow the soil and mulch to get mixed up.

Wide columns of yew are used to give structure to the Oudolf's garden in Hummelo, eastern Netherlands. Grasses are combined with perennials to contribute structure and texture.

Maintaining borders

The great herbaceous borders of Edwardian Britain established this kind of planting as an art form, but they did little for its reputation as something that everyone could achieve. Relying on plants that needed a lot of attention, such as Michelmas daisies (*Aster novi-belgii* hybrids), there was an endless, annual round of manuring, staking, weeding and dividing. The Karl Foerster tradition, on the other hand, relied far more on plants that were robust and did not need so much more attention.

Mixed borders (with shrubs) evolved in the way that they did partly because of the need to avoid too much maintenance. Contemporary border styles that almost entirely use perennials, stress the importance of relying on varieties that are robust and low-maintenance. They are able to survive for years without needing to be dug up and divided, do not require an annual fix of a high-nutrient feed and are sufficiently robust to stand up without any staking.

How much work a border requires depends on the choice of plants. More traditional English-style borders with a lot of roses, and perennials with a high-nutrient requirement, such as delphiniums, or seasonal plants, such as dahlias and annuals, require regular feeding if they are to thrive. The traditional practice of heaping on plenty of well-rotted manure in the autumn is a well-established way of doing this. Alternatively, a mulch of garden compost can be used with a slow-release general fertilizer if the soil is not particularly fertile. A more modern variant is to use a shredder to break down dead perennial stems, and pruning clippings, as an autumn mulch.

Part of the philosophy of a contemporary perennial border is that it should be planned with the soil type in mind. If it is poor, use varieties that do not need feeding, such as low-growing and colourful *Salvia nemorosa* and *Geranium sanguineum*. Whatever happens, do not feed taller plants because they might become top-heavy and flop over.

Allium
sphaerocephalon,
Perovskia and
Macleaya cordata
catch the evening sun
in a naturalistic
planting by Noël
Kingsbury

Cutting back

Two tasks dominate the annual maintenance regime of perennial-dominated borders: cutting back dead growth and weeding. In the past, perennials were cut back in the autumn leaving an unattractive expanse of bare earth, but current thinking favours leaving them standing, at least those with interesting structure, until late winter. Regions which have regular hoar frosts will see some spectacular displays as the frost leaves a magic layer of crystals on every surface, while garden birds will be grateful for the seeds and insects left behind in the dead stems. Shrubs may also need pruning, and this is generally done after flowering, but if more drastic pruning is needed, this is best done in the autumn or winter.

Further weeding

In addition to the weeding before planting, it is vital to keep an eye out for weeds throughout the year. Modern thinking aims to have a dense carpet of plants by late spring, so that there is no bare earth left for weed seedlings to colonize; if anything does appear after this, it will need to be pulled out by hand.

In regions with a mild winter there is usually a period between mid-winter and mid-spring when weed seedlings do appear, and grasses in particular start to cover the ground, especially if a mulch has not been used. It is important that they are hoed off before they get established. Perennial weeds regenerating from buried roots are more problematic; the best way to deal with them is with careful use of a glyphosate-based weedkiller that will kill their root systems but leave other plants unharmed. The chemical is inactivated as soon as it touches the soil, and is then broken down by bacteria.

Pests and diseases

We now have a more relaxed attitude to pests and
diseases than in the past. Pests and diseases are always
very specific, and since modern plantings involve a wide
mix of plants, this means that even if one species falls
victim then there are plenty of others that will continue to
look good. A good mixture of species also restricts the
ability of pests and diseases to spread.

However, slugs and snails can do enormous damage to
certain plants very early in the season, just as the new
leaves are emerging. Even in the wild they can cause local
extinctions. There are various products on the market
designed to tackle the problem. The most effective means
of control is the traditional slug pellet. Claims that the
pellets are harmful to wildlife appear to be largely
groundless, with a virtual absence of research studies
supporting the belief that they are hazardous. However on
a precautionary note it still makes sense to minimize their
use. Research shows that they only need be used very
sparingly: 10 pellets per 1 sq m (1 sq yd) every three weeks,
before the plants have filled out for the season, is all that is
required.

The yellow border in the old kitchen garden at Hadspen House, with a variety of yellow flowers and folige, is the most thoroughly planned one-colour border at Hadspen, and reflects Nori and Sandra Pope's belief that through its relationship to green, yellow is a harmonious colour

The experts' dos and don'ts on making borders

Do not concentrate on colour

Piet Oudolf is particularly worried that new gardeners concentrate on colour at the expense of other factors. But structure is equally important. Take a black and white photograph of your border and see what it looks like without the distractions of colour. The structure (or lack of) really stands out. In fact, many borders will seem an undifferentiated mass, while those with good structure will look almost as good in black and white as they do in colour. John Brookes' plans in particular show how effective a concentration on plant form can be.

Avoid too many shrubs

Many of the shrubs sold in garden centres can become very large with time, overwhelming smaller borders or even whole gardens. Piet Oudolf's designs are particularly refreshing because they largely do without shrubs. This is partly for reasons of space, but also because of what Piet sees as their amorphous shapes that contribute little to the structure of the planting, and their absence of colour after flowering. Penelope Hobhouse, a great believer in shrubs, especially evergreens, adds that many gardeners are wrong to imagine that shrubs are automatically low-maintenance. They most certainly are not if they are too big for the site and constantly need cutting back.

If you do have an established shrub that is too big for its site, note that it can be ruthlessly cut back, to ground level if need be. Despite what many think, shrubs are rarely killed by doing this, and the results are often a rejuvenated plant with better looking foliage and a neater habit.

Designed by Rupert Golby, the rose garden at the Old Rectory, Sudborough, features purple sage, *Salvia officinalis* 'Purpurea', the seed heads of *Allium christophii* and the sparse mauve flowers of *Verbena bonariensis*

Small spaces need big plants

Tall or big plants are particularly effective in small spaces. Build a border around one or two majestic plants and they will have real impact, whereas filling it with miniatures will constantly remind you how small it is. John Brookes' designs are particularly effective at making use of strong plants in small areas. Penelope Hobhouse stresses how height is important in small or city gardens, with verticals adding a new element to a flat space, while trees and pergolas create light and shade.

Avoid bare ground

Aim to have total soil coverage by late spring, and there will be much less space for invading weeds. Ground-covering or clumping perennials, for example the hardy geraniums and the popular *Stachys byzantina* with its wooly, silvery leaves, are particularly good choices for ground cover. A mulch of wood chips can be used to cover the soil, blocking out weeds, especially in the early stages. The gravel used by the Popes and John Brookes is another way to minimize maintenance because weed seeds rarely germinate in the stones. Gravel is also more stylish than chips, more durable over the long term and makes a good backdrop to a wide variety of flower colours.

Do not use too many different varieties

A large number of different plant varieties, especially if there is only one of each, creates an untidy and fussy border, something that was mentioned by all the designers. Such borders are little more than plant collections, the result of what John Brookes calls people 'thinking horticulturally rather than in design terms', while Nori Pope talks about 'people trying to compose a symphony when what is really needed is a chamber piece'. 'Less is more' is a motto that many gardeners should take to heart. Choose a few plants that you like, that look good with each other and succeed in your garden, and work with them.

In their different ways, I think all the contributors have adhered to this idea. John Brookes is a particularly strong exponent of this practice, which works well in conjunction with paving and brickwork. However, while he tends to clump together a few plants, I prefer to intermingle them, imitating the way plants grow in nature. John also suggests buying large perennials and splitting them up to produce several plants that can be either clumped to produce more impact, or repeated to create a satisfying rhythm through the border.

The Herb Garden at the Old Rectory, Sudborough , is framed by a wall of Lavender and full of aromatic herbs and flowers

Do not make borders too small

Far too many gardeners create borders that are just narrow strips. Several of the plans in this book are aimed at encouraging the reader to be bold and to plough up boring stretches of lawn, replacing them with wide borders that stretch right across the garden. The bigger the border the more you can try different effects and plant combinations.

Do not be discouraged by quirky, irregular areas or slopes

Small gardens are often odd shapes, but they are potentially more exciting than a rectangle. The best approach is to decide on one basic border feature that sets the tone for the whole garden, which could be a topiarized shrub or a collection of plants with strong scent or bold foliage.

Slopes can be off-putting, yet looking up at plants or down onto them offers a perspective that is all too rarely seen or appreciated. They do involve hard work, and need to be well planned to reduce maintenance as much as possible by using attractive plants that need little attention (see my plan for a low-maintenance planting on pages 126–129).

Avoid close planting

It is all too easy for new gardeners to pack plants together, but while this initially looks good, it creates long-term problems. Piet Oudolf also points out how easy it is to overcrowd plants in the spring when there is plenty of bare ground, creating the illusion that there is more space than really exists.

If you do want to create a full look very quickly, by all means overplant, but you must be prepared to be ruthless in future years, removing some plants to make room for others to grow and develop. Therefore make a clear distinction when planning between the priority plants that you want to keep, and less important fillers that could be removed later; alternatively, plant three of one particular variety, aiming to keep only one. The removed plants can be used elsewhere in the garden.

John Brookes

More than anyone else, John Brookes has helped turn garden design into a discipline, with his promotion of a professional body (the Society of Garden Designers) and numerous important books on the subject encouraging gardeners to understand the basic principles of planning and designing their plots. And, for many of us, his Chelsea Flower Show gardens of the 1980s and 1990s introduced us to contemporary garden design.

'I design garden *spaces*,' he says. 'Plants *per se* don't thrill me. My early experience working on the journal *Architectural Design* taught me that there had to be some sort of rules.' But while his early books and show gardens stressed the architect's eye, he now feels they over-emphasized structure leading many of us (myself included) to associate his work with bricks and patios. 'All I ever wanted to say,' he adds, 'was that a garden needs a structure despite the fact that it might then be lost in the planting.'

John began his career in commercial horticulture, then worked for three years with Nottingham Parks Department where he ended up in the design office. On leaving Nottingham, he sent some of his drawings to Brenda Colvin who, in the 1950s, was one of Britain's most notable landscape architects. She took him on and, after a university course, he moved on to work in the office of another big name in garden design, Sylvia Crowe. It was after this that he worked as a writer for *Architectural Design*. John then went freelance, since when he has

always balanced writing and lecturing with designing gardens for clients scattered over many countries, including France, Germany, Italy, the USA, Japan, Chile and Argentina.

Perhaps this international range of work has helped bring about the most recent change in John's approach, with great attention now being paid to what he calls the cultural element in horticulture – the importance of relating gardens to the local landscape, and using native plant associations if possible. He is worried that gardens around the world will look increasingly similar if we all grow the same plants.

Not surprisingly, given his architectural bent, John likes formality and structure in gardens, 'not necessarily classical straight lines but fractured formality, Japanese gardens, some French gardens, the gardens of the contemporary Belgian designer Jacques Wirtz (whose formal schemes are a modern working of a traditional idiom), and Islamic gardens, for example those in southern Spain'. 'But,' he adds, 'I don't go to many gardens now and when I do, I see nothing but mistakes. What moves me is landscape and countryside such as around the Sussex Downs where I live. I'd be hard pushed to think of a garden that bowls me over.

'I'm also increasingly interested in leaves – their colour, shape and texture – and in leaving space between the plants so that they can be clearly seen.' Previously he was attracted to the more dramatic leaves of yuccas, phormiums and sumachs – 'that was when I was in my architectural phase – but now I love native, lime-loving wildflowers, and seeing box and yew in the woods. You can learn so much from looking at how wildflowers grow, even if you do not actually use them'.

But it is important to look at the architectural element in John's work, and one way of tackling it is to relate it to the modern movement in art and architecture. John has often been seen as 'a modernist', a label he now rejects, but there is little doubt that one of the reasons for his importance as a garden designer is his relationship to the movement that started with the Bauhaus in the 1930s that favoured clarity of purpose and simplicity in design. In fact, the modern movement passed Britain by and had relatively little effect on garden design, unlike other art forms. But it did influence some garden designers, for example the Brazilian Roberto Burle Marx who, with his bold sweeps of planting and dramatic contrasts of colour and form, was the most prolific and best known proponent in a variety of rural and urban settings.

Talking of modernism, John says: 'I went through a lot of it... it set me up for life, but I am not a minimalist.' He adds, though, that he was influenced by the 'very simple clear cut lines' of Thomas Church's gardens, created during the 1940s and 1950s in California, which so successfully linked house, garden and landscape.

An interest in Islamic gardens has also been an important part of John's life. He describes researching them as 'a hobby of mine', which he indulged in during the 1960s and 1970s, starting off in southern Spain, moving on to Iran and then the Indian sub-continent. His resulting book, *Gardens of Paradise* (Weidenfeld & Nicolson, 1987), remains one of the few modern works that discusses the gardens and landscape of the Muslim world. Reading it now, it comes across as something that was written at a time when dialogue between cultures was easier, and there was more possibility of interesting international work being carried out in the Middle East. The book contains much valuable writing on the basic principles of the Islamic garden and on the general problems of gardening in a semi-desert climate, and one hopes that it will continue to inspire gardeners and designers in the future.

John's own garden at Denmans, near Arundel in West Sussex, has 3.5 acres (1.4 ha) of lawn, trees and carefully orchestrated foliage. Wandering around the garden one bright June day, I felt that I was exploring a very different kind of garden. I stress the word 'wandering' because it does not have any obvious axes or features to propel you in certain directions, something that is emphasised by the flatness of the surrounding countryside, just visible from a few views in the garden.

What first impressed me were the striking plant forms, but not the fashionable, spiky phormiums and yuccas seen everywhere. I loved the perennials with strong shapes such as the verbascums, with their distinctive rosettes and tall spires of yellow flowers, and various species of thistle-like eryngium. John told me how he prefers to 'work down from structure...colour is the last thing, a bonus'.

Yet the strong shapes never overwhelmed because they act as a counterpoint to the many mounds created by the hummocks of sage (*Salvia officinalis*), the low evergreen *Viburnum davidii* and the roughly-textured leaves of *Phlomis russeliana*. There are also many evergreens, many with Mediterranean-type grey leaves, as well as more traditional box. Some of the plants are clipped into dramatically large boulders that add structure and rhythm to an area of looser herbaceous and shrub planting.

What is interesting at Denmans is how few of those quintessentially contemporary plants, the ornamental grasses, he uses. He confesses that 'I have problems with them. I can't make them work in design terms'. As a result he has created a modern, grass-free garden where the prevalence of rounded shapes makes it feel much more Mediterranean in spirit. And the distinctive use of gravel reinforces the Mediterranean atmosphere, with a great river of it wending its way across the grass at one end of the garden, crossed by a stylized wooden bridge.

Since the gravel is part-footway and part-planting area, the edges between the two are blurred, often by plants seeding themselves into the gravel. Here and elsewhere, much of the planting is notably looser than is conventional. This allows well-shaped plants to be appreciated more fully than had they been squeezed into a border. Leaving space for plants to 'spread themselves spontaneously by self-sowing' is also important. Areas of gravel encourage this process, and they also have 'a looser, more informal feeling than grass'.

To me, Denmans evokes a series of open, woodland glades. While walking around I went from sun to shade and back again, with small groups of trees providing shady patches, but they were never so dense as to obstruct the view. Most of the trees are smaller species or have light

foliage, and include birches, *Gleditsia triacanthos* and *Robinia pseudoacacia*, all big enough to define spaces while allowing views through at eye level to another open patch of garden beyond.

John has lived at Denmans for about 25 years, but only owned it for the last 10. He came here 'because I liked it, and I was a friend of Joyce Robinson, the then owner, who made the original garden. She was a plantswoman,' says John, 'while I tried to iron out the garden, giving it a simpler design.' Interestingly, John has treated Denmans as if it was a private rather than a client's garden, by which he means 'I never made big positive decisions right at the start, though I did put the pond in; everything else has been added piecemeal'. The little changes here and there, over the years, have gently re-moulded one person's garden into another's.

This is how most gardeners develop their own gardens, and is perhaps a warning that designing your own garden in one go is not such a good idea. The message is clearly that designing a garden is a continual process that has to respond to many factors, including the way in which the plants grow and often die, so creating new possibilities.

Being such a clear and schematic thinker, it is instructive to listen to John describe the different processes of garden design. 'First of all,' he says, 'I decide on mood and character, and try to see things through my client's eye

often with a vague idea of colour. Then I go through the plant categories and make a selection.' He stresses how plantings have to relate to the proportion of the design, and how they will be seen against a backdrop of trees. Then he begins work on the 'skeleton material, moulding the design, building up massed shapes using cotoneasters and viburnums, etc., before moving on to a decorative range of plants, not doing one border at a time, but a bit here and there'. Finally come 'the pretties with perennials, smaller bulbs, sub-shrubs, such as lavender, and finally the infillers like bulbs'. He sums up his work by saying that a strong and simple framework is vital. 'Keep it simple,' he says, 'repeat plants, take out half of what you first thought of, and double up what is left . . . less is more.'

One of his final points is that a garden design must have a relationship to its surroundings. And it is this relationship – dubbed 'visual ecology' – that has most concerned him over the last few years. It is a two-way relationship involving the effect that the garden has on the surroundings, and the reflection of the local environment in the garden. This relationship should not be destroyed by creating, for example, a cottage garden in a modern city centre. In his recent book (*The New Garden*, Dorling Kindersley, 1998), he stresses the importance of local inspiration for the design and the need to repeat elements of the landscape in the garden, softening boundaries, and bringing views into the garden.

The mullein, *Verbascum bombyciferum*, self-sows into the gravel path that runs through this border, making an effective contrast with more amorphous plant shapes and generating a powerful sense of rhythm

John Brookes' use of plants to
structure garden spaces has
made him internationally
renowned

A lifelong commitment to clear, simple design has been the
hallmark of John's work, and the core message of the
modern gardening movement. He is distinctive amongst
British designers of his generation in not being a
traditionalist, with little interest in the historical revivalism
or eclecticism that has marked the work of many. And,
unlike many 20th-century British designers, he has not
tied his career to that of the big country house, and to the
essentially backward-looking values of the traditional
land-owning aristocracy who still dominate much British
aspiration, in gardening above all else. Freed from the ties
of tradition, he has been more international in outlook,
and perhaps more clear thinking. Above all he has helped,
and continues to help, move garden design into the 21st
century.

[Left] *Hibiscus syriacus*

[Right] *Eremurus robustus*

[Below] *Hedera Helix*
'Goldheart'

A tropical-inspired border

plant list

1. *Helenium* 'Moerheim Beauty'   (5)
2. *Campsis* × *tagliabuana* 'Madame Galen' (1)
3. *Ligularia dentata* 'Desdemona'   (3)
4. *Hosta fortunei* 'Gold Standard'   (7)
5. *Hemerocallis* 'Pink Sundae'   (6)
6. *Lysimachia nummularia* 'Aurea'   (12)
7. *Sedum telephium* subsp. *maximum* 'Atropurpureum' (6)
8. *Iris foetidissima* 'Variegata'   (4)
9. *Salvia officinalis* 'Icterina'   (3)
10. *Lychnis* × *arkwrightii*   (6)
11. *Angelica gigas*   (3)
12. *Hibiscus syriacus* 'Dorothy Crane'   (2)
13. *Canna* 'Di Bartolo'   (8)
14. *Hedera helix* 'Goldheart'   (1)
15. *Eremurus* hybrids   (23)
16. *Tulipa* 'Queen of Sheba'   (25)

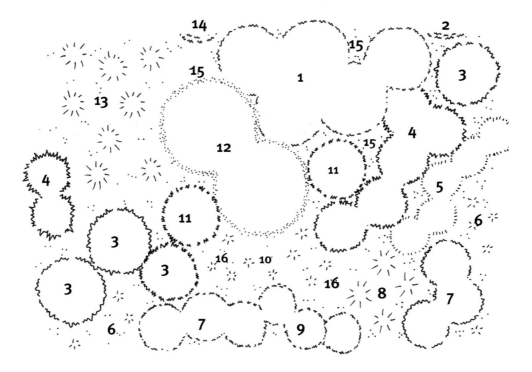

What is tropical is in the eye of the beholder. John believes that 'it involves leaf shape and colour, and strong flower colours' but maintains that 'to create the effect in a temperate climate will be something of a pastiche'. Given that many plants with especially distinctive foliage shapes or strong flowers are not particularly hardy, he warns that the plants need to be selected carefully. 'The important thing is to get that tropical clash of colour,' he says, adding 'I love that jungly look.'

He uses two *Hibiscus syriacus* 'Dorothy Crane', exotic-looking white flowers with a red centre, to provide the shrubby bulk at the core of this planting. In early summer a clump of eremurus hybrids thrust their spires skywards, each one packed with thousands of little orange and yellow flowers, while at the front there is a group of the lily-flowered tulip 'Queen of Sheba' with its yellow-edged orange flowers.

At its best during midsummer, the dominant colour theme of this planting is salmon-purple, backed up by a striking combination of foliage colours. The big, gold-leaved *Hosta fortunei* 'Gold Standard' and an underplanting of creeping yellow-leaved *Lysimachia nummularia* 'Aurea' contrast with the purple leaves and orange flowers of *Lychnis* × *arkwrightii*, and the purple foliage of *Angelica gigas* and *Sedum telephium* subsp. *maximum* 'Atropurpureum'.

Midsummer sees the deep red-orange of *Campsis* × *tagliabuana* 'Madame Galen' create a striking backdrop on the wall or fence behind. *Canna* 'Di Bartolo' has a strong colour, combining bronze leaves with deep pink flowers, and is a striking foliage plant that instantly evokes a feeling of the tropics wherever it is planted. With *Ligularia dentata* 'Desdemona', which also combines dramatic foliage and flowers, it is the dominant element in this planting through the summer. 'Desdemona' has jagged

REQUIREMENTS

edged, dark mahogany-green leaves and tall, branching heads of orange daisies. The dark purple umbels of *Angelica gigas* make a striking contrast. The rusty brown daisy-like flowers of *Helenium* 'Moerheim Beauty' bring the summer to a close.

During the winter the yellow-leaved ivy, *Hedera helix* 'Goldheart', maintains something of this planting's strong colour, as do the cream-streaked evergreen *Iris foetidissima* 'Variegata' and the golden-leaved sage, *Salvia officinalis* 'Icterina'.

1. With such strong colours it should be obvious that this is a planting that needs full sun to look its best. The campsis also needs a warm site, preferably against a sunny wall, for its growth to ripen well enough to flower regularly. The only plant that is not hardy is the canna; in mild districts its roots can be covered with a thick mulch to keep out the cold, otherwise it needs to be dug up and the tops cut off, with the rhizomes being stored inside, in a dry, cool frost-free place; replant next spring as the weather warms up.

2. Any reasonably fertile soil, preferably moister rather than drier, will suit the plants. The eremurus needs drier conditions, being a semi-desert plant; also avoid over-crowding.

3. *Angelica gigas* is a biennial, which means seed needs to be sown every year to produce flowers the following year. If you are lucky though, it might self-seed and do the job for you. *Lychnis* × *arkwrightii* is also short-lived, but freely self- seeds. The tulips rarely flower reliably from one year to another, and may need annual replacement.

4. The hosta and ligularia are prone to slug and snail attacks, the spring damage leaving the plants with unsightly holes for the rest of the season. Surrounding the plants with material the molluscs cannot cross, such as egg shells and bark chippings, can help avoid this.

5. Long-term, this planting should cause few problems in its management.

[Left] *Taxus baccata*
'Fastigiata Aurea'

[Right] *Viburnum davidii*

A foliage border for a small town garden

plant list

1. *Cynara cardunculus* (2)
2. *Buddleia davidii* (1)
3. *Jasminum nudiflorum* (1)
4. *Hydrangea villosa* (1)
5. *Taxus baccata* 'Fastigiata Aurea' (1)
6. *Santolina pinnata* subsp. *neopoltana* (6)
7. *Agapanthus* 'Headbourne Hybrids' (5)
8. *Heuchera micrantha* var. *diversifolia* 'Palace Purple' (3)
9. *Viburnum davidii* (2)
10. *Lilium regale* (8)
11. *Hedera helix* 'Goldheart' (1)
12. *Pittosporum tobira* 'Variegata' (1)
13. *Solanum crispum* 'Glasnevin' (1)
14. *Camellia* 'White Swan' (2)
15. *Rosa* 'Albéric Barbier' (1)

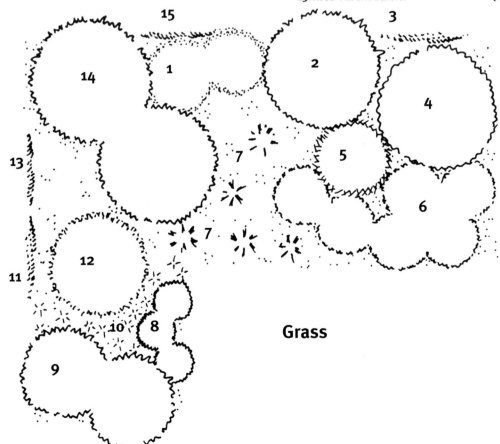

Grass

'This planting,' says John, 'is about furnishing the garden with greenery which I think is more important than flower colour.' One could argue that this is true for any garden, but it is absolutely essential for small town gardens where the freshness of foliage is always at a premium. And small gardens everywhere need to provide interest for as long as possible. Flowers are relatively short-lived and cannot be relied on to provide interest for long.

That is why evergreens form the bulk of this border. An upright Irish yew (*Taxus baccata* 'Fastigiata Aurea') provides a major focus of interest, and is balanced by two of the spring-flowering *Camellia* 'White Swan'. In front of the yew is the low growing, grey-leaved evergreen *Santolina pinnata* subsp *neapolitana* that provides a contrast in foliage colour. The *Pittosporum tobira* 'Variegata', by the side of the camellias, gives year-round interest, and in summer produces masses of sweetly-scented flowers.

The *Hydrangea villosa* behind the yew has strikingly large leaves and pink flower heads in midsummer, while *Buddleia davidii* on the other side is a large shrub that has butterfly-attracting violet flowers. There are a great many cultivars of the buddleia to choose from. The *Agapanthus* 'Headbourne Hybrids' are among the hardiest of these blue-flowering perennials; the strap-like leaves make an effective ground cover, filling gaps between the shrubs.

The dark leaves of *Heuchera micrantha* var. *diversifolia* 'Palace Purple' act as an edging on the other side of the planting, creating a good foil for the creamy-white *Lilium regale*. And *Viburnum davidii*, at the end of this part of the border, is a low-growing shrub with elegant, evergreen leaves and dark berries.

The most dramatic plant here is the perennial *Cynara cardunculus*. There are two in the centre creating a major attraction from spring onwards as their very large, grey, and deeply-toothed leaves begin to emerge, culminating in a dramatic, thistle-like blue flower during summer.

Being surrounded by walls on two sides, there is some scope for climbers. They include the yellow-leaved *Hedera helix* 'Goldheart', *Solanum crispum* 'Glasnevin' with its purple 'potato flowers' in mid- to late summer, the fragrant creamy-coloured rose 'Alberic Barbier' and the winter flowering *Jasminum nudiflorum*.

REQUIREMENTS

1. The plants need full sun, at least for most of the day, and any reasonable soil, although the camellia will not be happy in very hot sites or on thin or alkaline soils.

2. The pittosporum and the solanum are the least hardy. The santolina is best maintained by pruning after flowering, to encourage compact growth.

3. Several of the woody plants can become very large with time, which could ruin the balance and overall feel of the planting. The yew may need trimming to keep it from becoming too bushy, while the buddleias are notorious for getting far too big far too quickly, unless they are cut to ground level every winter; do not worry, they will still make 2–3m (6–9ft) growth in the summer and flower well.

A shady foliage planting

plant list

1. *Primula vulgaris* (153)
2. *Cyclamen hederifolium* (20)
3. *Iris foetidissima* (4)
4. *Helleborus foetidus* (5)
5. *Geranium sylvaticum* 'Mayflower' (29)
6. *Symphytum* × *uplandicum* (3)
7. *Euphorbia amygdaloides* var. *robbiae* (12)
8. *Digitalis purpurea* 'Alba' (9)
9. *Pulmonaria officinalis* 'Cambridge Blue' (6)
10. *Alchemilla mollis* (4)
11. *Lilium pardalinum* (18)
12. *Narcissus* 'W. P. Milner' (100)

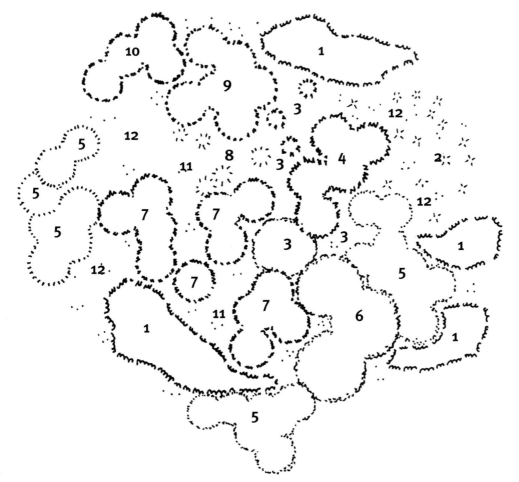

'Since my foliage planting is beneath a tree that casts only light shade, it is damp and not dry shade. Even so, there are several species here that will also do well in dry shade. The natural-looking planting is inevitably orientated to spring and autumn instead of summer.'

Of these *Euphorbia amygdaloides* var. *robbiae* can be invaluable in difficult shade. It has dark evergreen leaves and yellow-green flowers in early spring, and a spreading habit that can be a boon in large shady areas, but it can create problems in smaller ones. *Helleborus foetidus* and *Iris foetidissima* are also evergreens that are reasonably tolerant of drier shade. The hellebore is one of those rare plants that looks best in winter, forming a great mound of rather elegantly divided leaves topped by pale green flowers. The iris has dark, strap-shaped leaves and clusters of orange berries that usually last well through the winter.

Early spring sees the blue flowers of *Pulmonaria officinalis* 'Cambridge Blue' and the pale yellow of several patches of the primrose, *Primula vulgaris*, with the soft yellow flowers of an early daffodil, *Narcissus* 'W. P. Milner'. By late spring the clear blue comfrey, *Symphytum* × *uplandicum*, is in flower, and by early summer there is the violet-blue *Geranium sylvaticum* 'Mayflower', that is followed by the yellow-green *Alchemilla mollis*.

A little later the foxglove, *Digitalis purpurea* 'Alba', produces its tall spikes of white flowers, bringing light into the shade. *Lilium pardalinum*, an unusual orange lily that thrives in damp shade, also flowers in the early to midsummer period. In late summer, *Cyclamen hederifolium* starts to flower, its pink flowers like a miniature version of the Christmas pot plant. While the period after midsummer is relatively flowerless, there is a good selection of different foliage textures and shapes.

[Left] *Euphorbia amygdaloides* var. *robbiae*

[Right] *Digitalis purpurea* '**Alba**'

REQUIREMENTS

1. Any reasonable soil that does not badly dry out in summer will suit all these plants. However, several are quite tolerant of dryish shade, as noted.

2. The digitalis is very short lived but nearly always self-seeds; some of the seedlings will be pink, and this colour will reassert itself over several generations. Pink-flowering seedlings can usually be distinguished from the white ones because they have more of a red flush on the leaves. *Helleborus foetidus* is a relatively short-lived plant too, but also self-seeds well. The geranium also spreads through seedings.

3. The euphorbia and symphytum can be invasive, particularly on fertile soils, which can cause problems; ensure that they are given plenty of space.

4. Since several of these plants self-sow, and therefore change their positions from year to year (some are very vigorous spreaders), this planting may well change from year to year quite considerably. Take care that the less vigorous ingredients, such as the pulmonaria, are not swamped, and that the most vigorous (impossible to predict) do not take over entirely. A firm controlling, weeding hand is vital.

61

A contemporary mixed planting

plant list

1. *Artemisia* 'Powis Castle'   (4)
2. *Allium giganteum*   (14)
3. *Lavatera thuringiaca* 'Barnsley'   (2)
4. *Helictotrichon sempervirens*   (2)
5. *Allium aflatunense*   (15)
6. *Iris* 'Blue Denim'   (4)
7. *Rosa* 'Mutabilis'   (3)
8. *Salvia officinalis* 'Purpurascens'   (4)
9. *Perovskia atriplicifolia* 'Blue Spire'   (3)
10. *Tulipa*, lily-flowered, white   (25)
11. *Potentilla fruticosa* 'Katherine Dykes'   (5)
12. *Sisyrinchium striatum*   (6)
13. *Phormium tenax*   (2)
14. *Iris germanica* 'Golden Alps'   (3)
15. *Kniphofia caulescens*   (4)
16. *Ceanothus thyrsiflorus* var. *repens*   (1)

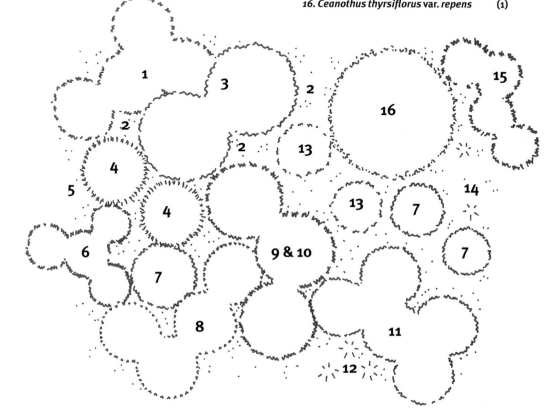

'I haven't defined the medium of the hard landscaping that surrounds this planting because I would like the look to be fluffy at the edges, so that there is no strict line between the border and path,' says John, but it will need to be gravel, shingle or another hard, loose material. One of the unusual and attractive features about John's own garden, in West Sussex, is the way that his gravel paths and plantings in gravel do merge into each other. Redefining accepted conventions is part of his contemporary style.

So too is his move away from perennials and grasses, unlike many modern designers, towards shrubs. He says that, being 'increasingly in Britain, I'm getting a bit bored with perennials and grasses because the joy of the English climate, I believe, is our capacity to grow shrubby plants well'.

This design includes shrubby plants and a central role for strong foliage shapes, a key ingredient of modern designs. Note the rosettes of *Kniphofia caulescens*, a dramatic clump of *Phormium tenax*, bearded iris cultivars, and the iris-like leaves of the *Sisyrinchium striatum,* all of which contrast with the mound-like forms of *Ceanothus thyrsiflorus* var. *repens, Salvia officinalis* 'Purpurascens', *Rosa* 'Mutabilis' and *Lavatera thuringiaca* 'Barnsley'.

The scattering of the ornamental onions, *Allium giganteum* and *A. aflatunense*, with their tall drumstick-like flower heads, and the grass *Helictotrichon sempervirens*, with its superb seed heads, add further seasonal elements to the picture. Many of these plants are evergreen or semi-evergreen, with a variety of foliage colours ranging from the dark green of the ceanothus to the purple of the salvia and the silver of *Artemisia* 'Powis Castle'.

The year starts in late spring with white lily-flowered tulips and the purple alliums, followed by blue and yellow irises in early summer, when the scene is dominated by the masses of blue ceanothus flowers. The rose has flowers that quickly change colour from yellow to orange and red, while the sisyrinchium and potentilla are both primrose yellow. The kniphofia's flowers, like the rose's, turn colour as they age, in this case from red to yellow, and generally appear later in the summer while the perovskia's are misty blue-mauve in midsummer. The lavatera flowers profusely all summer with dark pink-eyed, white flowers. Having gravel around these plants will act as a marvellous foil for the different colours, and makes an effective mulch, locking moisture in the ground in dry periods.

REQUIREMENTS

1. Any reasonable well-drained soil will suit these plants, as will any open site that is sheltered from cold winter or spring winds. Cold winters may cut the lavatera to ground level, but it soon recovers. It may occasionally produce branches with pink flowers, and the former must be cut off before more appear and take over.

2. The lavatera is never a long-lived plant, with five years being a reasonable life-span, and the ceanothus may die after 10 years. Also note that both grow very big, as does the phormium, and they should be given plenty of space at the outset. However, this can create temporary problems, because there will initially be gaps to the sides before the plants fill out. Solve the problem using alliums and the sisyrinchiums as temporary fillers, to be removed when the gaps start closing. Once the lavatera and ceanothus die you will have to decide whether to replace them with the same species or try something different.

3. The alliums and the sisyrinchiums can self-sow on some soils, adding a note of spontaneity; indeed the sisyrinchium can sometimes almost become a weed.

[Left] *Perovskia atriplicifolia* 'Blue Spire'

[Centre] *Artemisia* 'Powis Castle'

[Right] *Ceanothus thyrsiflorus* var. *repens*

This deep, full border at
the Old Rectory,
Sudborough,
demonstrates Rupert
Golby's belief that gardens
shouldn't look as if they
have been designed, but
have evolved

Rupert Golby

'The biggest complement anyone can pay me,' says Rupert Golby, 'is to say that it doesn't look like you've had a designer in here.' One of the younger generation of garden designers, his approach to design is subtle and plant orientated. He says that he likes to think of himself 'as really just gardening for the future', and that he would 'rather approach a garden through plants than through design'. For Rupert, design is very much an extension of horticulture rather than a separate activity.

In many ways, Rupert is working at the very heart of the English gardening tradition, both geographically because he is based in the Cotswolds, home of Hidcote and Kiftsgate, two of the best-loved and most influential English gardens, and metaphorically because he adopts a traditional approach. Nearly all his clients are private, many with historic houses and gardens, although he has also carried out a major restoration project for English Heritage, at Osborne House on the Isle of Wight, working on the walled kitchen garden.

He took up gardening at the age of four when he started growing hollyhocks, and went on to study at the Royal Horticutural Society's Garden at Wisley, and then the Royal Botanic Garden at Kew, both in the UK. One of his first jobs was at Ninfa, in Italy, a romantic garden built around the ruins of a town: 'An extraordinary garden,' he says, 'and a great influence.' Rosemary Verey, for whom he also worked, was another crucial influence. 'She used plants as a painter would, almost without regard for the fact that

they are plants. They were there to be exploited, not tended, which was quite an eye-opener to me.' Rupert also mentions Christopher Lloyd as a source of inspiration. 'I like his unorthodox use of plants ... what looks like neglect is in fact intended. By which I mean, for example, his love of dying fern fronds and old lawns seeded with wild flowers.'

Rupert's credo is that: 'A garden has to take its reference from the house.' Once away from the house the garden 'should not creep into the countryside'. He also 'likes to furnish a house with climbers, using multiple plantings growing together, making a billowy rather than a rigorously pruned look'.

Balance and harmony are obviously very important to Rupert, and it is interesting to notice how much symmetry there is in his plans. He adds that he dislikes strong colours because: 'I find them artificial and prefer a tapestry effect.' He is fond of using big blocks of plants in certain places, for example *Acanthus mollis* across the front of a house, but also of creating 'a speckled effect over a large area' by mixing three or so individuals of one particular species.

Evergreens play an important role in Rupert's work, indeed his own house is easily recognized by the big clipped hollies that stand sentinel outside the front door. 'Clients,' he says, 'are increasingly demanding year-round interest, and are more and more intolerant of plants with just one season of interest — which is why I am using greater numbers of evergreens, such as phillyrea and sarcococca.' *Phillyrea angustifolia* is hardly new (it has been in cultivation since the 18th century), but it is now increasingly available because the Italian nursery trade is exporting it in growing numbers to Britain, a good example of how the commercial availability of plants affects garden design.

When designing a planting scheme, Rupert is emphatic that he starts with what the clients want, and that the design is negotiated with them at all stages. 'Then we have to decide what stays in the garden, and then set about linking the old and new plantings. It is also important to decide if an area is to have a short, intense period of interest or a diluted interest over a longer period.'

He finds that most of his clients want a traditional look, and any temptation he has to try something more contemporary inevitably succumbs to the client's desire to play safe. Either that or the architecture of the 'new pseudo-Georgian houses' does not lend itself to anything experimental. He adds: 'I work for a lot of wealthy clients, including a lot of rock stars, who you think would want to be contemporary, but in fact they all want a traditional stone house, and that sets the tone of the garden. All rebel rock stars slot back into wanting the traditional signs of wealth. People,' he continues, 'want restful, peaceful gardens, nothing shocking or jarring, though I try to include some modern ideas.' One relatively recent development is that Rupert finds most of his clients want entertainment venues, like areas for furniture, barbecues etc., incorporated in their gardens; a sign perhaps that the 'garden for living in' concept, pioneered by Thomas Church in 1950s California, really has arrived in Britain.

[Left] The colours of the flowers and foliage in this border have been limited to white, silver and blue with hot pink cosmos for contrast

[Right] Herbs and perennials spill over the path through the pottager at the Old Rectory

Rupert is adamant that he is contemporary because: 'I use many of the huge range of plants that are now available. I like to see unusual or new plants used on a large scale, not just as single specimens. For example, I worked on a garden in Dorset where we put in a whole avenue of cut-leaved beech, *Fagus sylvatica* 'Aspleniifolia'.' His use of tender perennials is also very contemporary. He likes to integrate them with herbaceous plants in borders, salvias, argyranthemums and dahlias, but sometimes uses them on their own. 'They might be weak in early summer,' he says, 'but they are so startling at the end of summer.'

The increasingly popular grasses though, are not necessarily his favourite plants. 'The best way of using them is in terrific quantities, and they can look good with perennials but they look misplaced with shrubs. The main problem is that they are so often dotted around as a gesture.' The use of newly available plants is one way in which an old garden can be 'made to look forward', which Rupert thinks is much better than 'just slavishly putting in plants of the period, and anyway gardens die if you simply preserve them'.

Rupert's view of gardens is that they do not improve as they age (as everyone thinks), but that they gradually die, and need rescuing before it is too late. Most of Rupert's work is in old gardens where there is no question of their being a blank slate; a sensitive approach is needed to restoration, thinning existing planting and making everything more manageable. Much of this work is actually 'very destructive, because gardens are often overplanted or have never been thinned, which is particularly the case with trees. And after thinning they often look so much better'. His sensitivity to plants and landscape is important as gardens are gradually remoulded. 'I do not want to use plants like building blocks, I'd rather make a happy garden rather than a building site. I believe in creating a balance, and that's when the garden becomes a magical place.'

Whether he is working on old or new gardens, he says he is finding that increasing numbers of clients want to take an organic approach to gardening, but without understanding the issues involved. Like most designers he finds it can be a problem. 'One of my biggest gardens is

[Left] Allium seedheads have been left in the rose garden at the Old Rectory to provide contrast of shape with the low mounds of purple sage and of colour with the deep red roses

[Right] A shady, green and white border that relies on foliage shape and colour will look good all year round

completely organic, and is a complete nightmare. We have so many gardens that were designed to be completely chemical dependent and that are now being run organically, but this approach is so labour-intensive and time-consuming. The key issue is the use of herbicides because unchecked weeds are the great enemy of ornamental plants in Britain.' Rupert reckons a good compromise 'is to clean up a garden with herbicides and then use organic methods after that'. Interestingly, several committed organic growers have said as much to me, strictly off the record of course.

Like many plant-influenced designers, Rupert stresses that 'how a garden is maintained is almost more important than the original design'. And the vast majority of clients do want Rupert to be involved after the project has been completed, often to create projects, but also to monitor the development of the garden and advise them and their staff. Advising gardeners can be tricky, but Rupert finds that 'almost without exception staff appreciate your input, but you do have to prove yourself by working along-side them'.

Besides paying attention to the plants, Rupert (like all designers) has to be involved intimately with the hard landscaping (including paving, stonework and timber, etc.). But the plants get all the attention. 'How often do you hear someone go into a garden and say "wonderful steps", after so much money and effort went into them?' 'But the truth is,' he says, 'that they are vital for each other.'

A discussion of hard landscaping inevitably leads towards talk about the latest developments in gardening, and the popular new shows at Chaumont-sur-Loire in France, and at Westonbirt Arboretum, in Gloucestershire, UK, where installation art meets garden design in a flurry of scaffolding poles, mirrors, coloured plastic sheeting, glass, gravel and new materials. Not surprisingly Rupert is lukewarm. 'It is good to be provocative, and it makes people think about what a garden really is, but it is important that the installations don't get in the way of real gardening. A lot of it does not contribute to gardening and some is an intrusion, and there is a danger that the plants could be sidelined.'

*Allium
sphaerocephalon*

Rupert concludes that 'gardening has changed out of all recognition in the last few years', especially with the growth of make-over TV programmes and media interest in the garden. 'People now feel chanelled into design, whereas in the past they were happy just gardening and growing things, and it was the process of growing that people enjoyed. Many of our greatest gardens were planted by enthusiastic amateurs.'

Perhaps in many ways Rupert represents the true heart of English gardening, someone who, while being aware of the latest trends, prefers to work in a more incremental way, building on what history has bequeathed us rather than going out of his way to plough new furrows. His deep understanding of plants is also something that is fundamental to English garden design.

The vast range of plants that will flourish in the climate of the British Isles means that designers have an almost overwhelming range of species to use, though very few of today's garden designers actually have the knowledge (or inclination) to use them effectively. This, with the fact that the climate of the British Isles is so weed-friendly, means that designers working here will arguably always need to be more horticulturally biased and skillful than in other countries. Whatever new trends affect garden design in Britain, it will always be practitioners like Rupert who will remain the bedrock of the profession.

A border of year-round interest

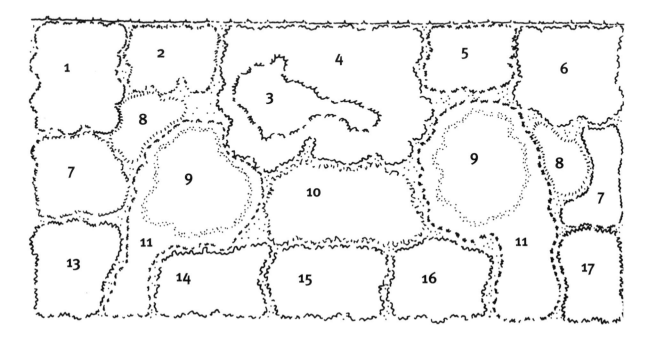

Magnolia grandiflora

Rupert says that having the plantings look good all year is a major priority of many for his clients. 'Borders adjacent to a house, where they are constantly seen, particularly need to be well furnished throughout the year, even in the depths of winter, without necessarily being flower strewn and colourful. It is more important that they should be healthy, well shaped and full.' Evergreens are therefore important, partly because they make 'such a satisfying block against which deciduous plants of winter interest are shown off to advantage, one of the best examples being the red-stemmed *Cornus alba* 'Elegantissima'.'

This particular border features a number of plants with lustrous green leaves at the back, although the foliage of the centrally-placed *Magnolia grandiflora* 'Exmouth' are an interestingly lighter shade, with brown undersides. Once established this species will produce occasional huge and scented white flowers in mid-summer. The osmanthus has deliciously scented white blossom in spring, the arbutus has white lily of the valley-like flowers in early summer followed by red, strangely strawberry-like fruit later, while the photinia has deep mahogany-red young growth in spring.

These evergreens provide a fine backdrop for the red stems of *Cornus alba* 'Elegantissima' in winter and for its cream variegated leaves in summer, and for the fine creamy-white flowers of the rambling rose 'Gardenia'. They need to be held against the wall on wires until the magnolia is large enough to offer support, when the rose can be encouraged to poke through its branches.

Around the cornus are clumps of *Iris foetidissima*, an iris with relatively inconspicuous flowers but striking orange berries in autumn that usually last well into winter, along with its dark green leaves. *Hebe* 'Mrs Winder' has contrasting bronze-purple foliage. Framing the central part of the planting are two plants – *Ruscus aculeatus* and *Blechnum tabulare* – that add considerably to the long season of structural interest. The ruscus has very stiff, dark green leafy stems and an ability to thrive in the most unpromising dry shade, while the blechnum is a fern with strikingly cut, leathery-looking leaves. The latter needs a site that never dries out, and will only really flourish in relatively mild climates. Other ferns, such as dryopteris and polystichum, would be suitable in colder situations.

[Left] *Helleborus foetidus*

[Centre] *Blechnum tabulare*

[Right] Seedheads of *Iris foetidissima*

The centrally-placed *Viburnum davidii* has a neat, low habit, with elegant evergreen leaves and dark blue berries, while *Sarcococca confusa* is another evergreen, low-growing, clump-forming shrub whose main feature is the scented winter flowers. The two species of helleborus are both primarily foliage plants, forming striking clumps of evergreen leaves topped by lime-green flowers in winter, while the bergenia has magenta flowers in early spring and large, red leaves that turn deep bronze-red in winter.

REQUIREMENTS

1. This border is suitable for any aspect other than north-facing, and needs shelter from cold winter winds. Any reasonable soil is fine.

2. All the plants used are notably long-lived; if not crowded and planted at suitable planting distances, many will still be there in 100 years time. The planting distances are crucial because many of the plants will take many years to reach their mature size. Avoid the temptation to plant them closer together than the distances given for their eventual spreads or the more vigorous species will block out the others.

Many of the shrubs along the rear of the border are large growers, but there is a danger that they might initially be planted too close together. If this happens they can be clipped or pruned, but the result may be rather artificial. Selective removal may be the best option.

A border with scented plants and herbs

plant list

1. *Buddleia alternifolia* 'Argentea' (3)
2. *Lonicera periclymenum* 'Cornish Cream' (3)
3. *Foeniculum vulgare* 'Purpureum' (3)
4. *Rosa rubiginosa* (1)
5. *Nepeta sibirica* 'Souvenir d'André Chaudron' (2)
6. *Perovskia atriplicifolia* (2)
7. *Artemisia ludoviciana* subsp. *ludoviciana* var. *latiloba* (2)
8. *Calamintha nepeta* (3)
9. *Rosmarinus officinalis* 'Benenden Blue' (6)
10. *Lilium candidum* (2)
11. *Dictamnus albus* (1)

12. *Hyssopus officinalis* (1)
13. *Thymus vulgaris* (4)
14. *Origanum laevigatum* (1)
15. *Cistus × cyprius* (1)
16. *Allium sphaerocephalon* (10)
17. *Phuopsis stylosa* (1)
18. *Nerine bowdenii* (10)
19. *Salvia officinalis* (2)
20. *Myrrhis odorata* (1)
21. *Euphorbia characias* 'Blue Hills' (1)
22. *Lilium regale* (2)
23. *Verbascum olympicum* (5)
24. *Aquilegia vulgaris* 'Belhaven Blue' (4)
25. *Eryngium alpinum* 'Amethyst' (1)
26. *Atriplex halimus* (1)

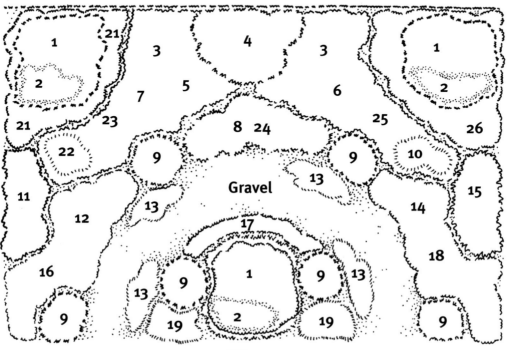

Lilium regale 'Album'

Getting access to fragrant plants is a vital part of this and, indeed, any planting. Consequently this border has a path that curves round allowing exploration right into the bed.

Rupert uses three semi-standard specimens of *Buddleia alternifolia* 'Argentea' that need regular pruning to retain their open, airy habit, and which provide the only element of regularity in this otherwise informal miscellany. His intention is that 'multiple plantings of herbaceous plants should run together and merge with neighbouring combinations to give a massed effect of form, colour and scent'.

Each buddleia is accompanied by a honeysuckle (*Lonicera periclymenum* 'Cornish Cream') which, until the buddleia is large enought to support it, will requite a tripod of canes, and an underplanting. The evergreen *Euphorbia characias* 'Blue Hills' used beneath one of the buddleias flowers very early in the year, with lime-green flowers, and its greyish leaves are echoed by those of the semi-evergreen, silvery leaves of the *Atriplex halimus* below one of the other buddleias. *Myrrhis odorata*, used beneath the third, is a sophisticated cow-parsley with deep green

filigree foliage and white flower heads in early summer. The rose is the sweet briar, with small pink flowers and long-lasting scarlet hips, its main feature being the apple-scented foliage.

Most of the other plants here are low-growing species, many of Mediterranean origin, their aromatic foliage being characteristic of the drought-resistant flora of this area. Some, such as rosemary, sage (*Salvia officinalis*), fennel (*Foeniculum vulgare* 'Purpureum') thyme, oreganum and hyssop, double as culinary herbs. Most are low-growing and sprawling, much of their charm arising from the fact that they will intermingle with each other and form irregular mats of foliage across the gravel path. *Phuopsis stylosa* is perhaps a brave choice because it has a strong smell in summer, reminiscent of garlic. Its deep pink flowers in early to midsummer are certainly striking.

Plants with a marked upright habit are very useful as a contrast to low-growing species. The list includes aquilegias, to flower in late spring and early summer, sumptuously scented white lilies (*Lilium candidum* and *L. regale*), the clustered white spikes of *Dictamnus albus*,

79

[Left] *Phuopsis stylosa*

[Right] *Buddleia alternifolia* 'Argentea'

the thistle-like *Eryngium alpinum* 'Amethyst' and, most dramatic of all, the tall spires of the mullein (*Verbascum olympicum*). *Perovskia atriplicifolia* also has an upright habit, but is less clearly defined. A number of bulbs also provide a contrast, and they include the dark red-pink of the midsummer flowering *Allium sphaerocephalon* and the bright pink *Nerine bowdenii* in autumn.

The predominant colours are white, blues and mauves, with the occasional pink. The use of gravel provides a good backdrop for these colours and low-maintenance ground cover.

REQUIREMENTS

1. Full sun and any reasonable well-drained soil will suit this scheme. Many will also do well on dry or sandy soils. Nerines, in particular, appreciate a hot spot.

2. Gravel's practical advantages are many: it reduces moisture loss and helps prevent weeds from gaining a foothold. However, it encourages some plants to self-sow; amongst the species used here, the verbascum, aquilegia, foeniculum, allium and *Lilium regale* will readily do so, creating attractive drifts. The loose surface also enables surplus seedlings and weeds to be easily pulled out.

3. This should be a successful long-term planting. Some species (the rosemary, cistus and salvia) might eventually become very woody and unattractive and need replacing. Others may die out (the verbascum and foeniculum) but invariably replace themselves with seedlings. Where plants eventually make large clumps they may detract from the design, but they can easily be divided and thinned out.

A border of bold foliage plants

plant list

1.	*Miscanthus sinensis* 'Gracillimus'	(1)
2.	*Eryngium pandanifolium*	(1)
3.	*Aralia elata*	(1)
4.	*Macleaya cordata*	(1)
5.	*Epimedium × versicolor* 'Sulphureum'	(3)
6.	*Acanthus mollis*	(5)
7.	*Sasa veitchii*	(1)
8.	*Angelica archangelica*	(1)
9.	*Phyllostachys nigra*	(2)
10.	*Levisticum officinale*	(1)

Wall

1 2 6 3 6 4 5 7 8 10 6 6 9 **Paving** 6 9

Rupert describes this border as 'a celebration of foliage, combining a broad spectrum of beautiful leaved plants'. It is ideal for a courtyard or enclosed space where year-round greenery is desired. Different shapes of foliage are contrasted with each other, the result being a very bold planting.

Aralia elata is at the centre and will dominate the planting when mature. It has very large, pinnate leaves and what Rupert calls 'lethally spiked' stems. He describes the *Acanthus mollis* around it as 'forming statuesque iconography'. It is semi-evergreen and is one of the most tolerant and resilient of those perennials that have very striking foliage, and is enhanced in summer by bold white and mauve flower spikes.

Eryngium pandanifolium is another bold perennial with lots of thistle-like flower heads and dramatically toothed leaves. It will be echoed by the similarly tall and bold angelica (*Angelica archangelica*) and lovage (*Levisticum officinale*) to the sides, all three being members of the cow-parsley family. *Macleaya cordata* in the right-hand

corner is also large, but it is a gentler looking plant with grey-toned leaves, vaguely resembling fig leaves, the colour being a good contrast with the strong greens of the other plants.

The *Miscanthus sinensis* 'Gracillimus' is an ornamental grass with elegant, plume-like flower and seed spikes from late summer until late winter. The two bamboos that frame the area are the black-stemmed *Phyllostachys nigra*, while the much shorter but broader leaved *Sasa veitchii* fills a corner of the paving. The opposite corner is planted with the perennial *Epimedium × versicolor* 'Sulphureum' that forms a dense clump of glossy, bronze-tinted leaves.

REQUIREMENTS

1. The majority of these plants are probably happiest in light shade, in soil that is well drained but does not regularly dry out.

2. Soil moisture is particularly important for the bamboos. Also note that since the *Sasa veitchii* bamboo can spread invasively when mature, you should surround its rooting area with slates, tiles or heavy duty plastic to keep it within bounds.

3. All the other plants are perennials apart from the angelica, which is usually biennial, so young plants need to be planted every year to ensure continuity; allow self-sown seedlings to fill their parents' places.

4. This planting should be long-lived, with competition between spreading clumps of plants the only long-term management problem; the acanthus, in particular, is a rather over-enthusiastic grower, especially in warmer sites.

[Left] *Acanthus spinosus*

[Right] *Miscanthus sinesis* 'Gracillimus'

A border of yellow and blue

plant list

1. *Bupleurum fruticosum* (4)
2. *Anthemis tinctoria* 'E.C. Buxton' (2)
3. *Euphorbia characias* subsp. *characias* 'Humpty Dumpty' (2)
4. *Nepeta govaniana* (1)
5. *Nigella damascena* (10)
6. *Campanula persicifolia* (3)
7. *Camassia leichtlinii* (10)
8. *Eryngium* × *oliverianum* (2)
9. *Linum perenne* (3)
10. *Achillea taygetea* (2)
11. *Clematis* × *durandii* (2)
12. *Ceanothus thyrsiflorus* var. *repens* (2)
13. *Clematis integrifolia* 'Pastel Blue' (1)
14. *Kniphofia* 'Little Maid' (4)
15. *Eryngium bourgatii* 'Picos Blue' (3)
16. *Iris pallida* 'Variegata' (5)
17. *Eryngium giganteum* (2)
18. Pot planted with *Solanum rantonnetii* and *Bidens ferulifolia* (1)
19. *Milium effusum* 'Aureum' (6)
20. *Parahebe perfoliata* (2)
21. *Hypericum olympicum* 'Sulphureum' (3)
22. *Veronica longifolia* 'Blauer Sommer' (3)
23. *Melissa officinalis* 'Aurea' (2)
24. *Sisyrinchium striatum* 'Aunt May' (1)
25. *Helictotrichon sempervirens* (2)
26. *Linum narbonense* (2)
27. *Polemonium caeruleum* (3)

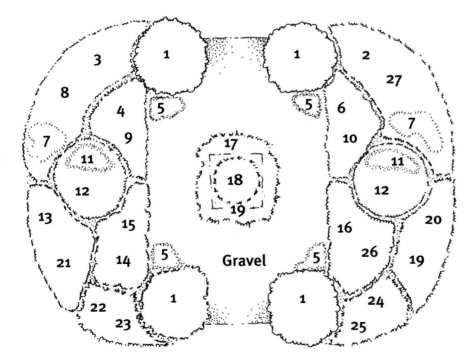

This plan for an island bed provides colour throughout the summer. The dominant theme is yellow (including many less common pale yellows) and blue, with a variety of interesting foliage shapes and textures. Rupert describes it as being 'held down by the use of evergreen shrubs with a low dome-like habit'. His two key plants in this respect are the *Ceanothus thrysiflorus* var. *repens* and *Bupleurum fruticosum*. The former has striking blue flowers in early summer, the latter has greeny-yellow flowers at roughly the same time. The fine texture of the former makes a good contrast with the larger, glossier leaves of the latter.

Early summer is particularly colourful with the blue camassias, *Campanula persicifolia*, the two linum species and *Polemonium caeruleum* in flower, while the pale yellow *Anthemis tinctoria* 'E. C. Buxton', *Nepeta govaniana* and *Hypericum olympicum* 'Sulphureum' will also be in flower. Slightly later, two species of blue eryngium start flowering, while *Kniphofia* 'Little Maid' has primrose yellow spikes of tightly packed tubular flowers, making it

one of the finest of the red hot pokers. Slightly paler is *Sisyrinchium striatum* 'Aunt May' with flowers in whorled spikes. It also has rather iris-like variegated foliage, echoing that of *Iris pallida* 'Variegata'.

The two clematis varieties provide plenty of blue interest throughout the summer: *Clematis* × *durandii* has dark purple blue flowers and a herbaceous scrambling habit, and can attractively drape itself over the ceanothus, neatly making the same space flower twice. *Clematis integrifolia* 'Pastel Blue' has small nodding flowers and, while not a climber, does need some support, for example using pea sticks.

A number of the plants have coloured or distinctive foliage. Both *Melissa officinalis* 'Aurea' and *Milium effusum* 'Aureum' are yellow tinted, which combines well with the blue flowers, while the grass *Helictotrichon sempervirens* has blue-grey leaves. *Parahebe perfoliata* also has greyish leaves, blue flowers and, like many Australian plants, a very singular appearance, with its leaves arranged on spreading, nodding stems.

REQUIREMENTS

The centre of the planting is gravelled where a raised pot of tender perennials gives added emphasis to the centre of the planting. He suggests using the dark blue-purple *Solanum rantonnetii* with the deep yellow *Bidens ferulifolia* to intensify the colour scheme. 'Miss Willmott's Ghost' (*Eryngium giganteum*) and the yellow grass *Milium effusum* 'Aureum' surround the pot, while the blue-flowered annual *Nigella damascena* is sown in the corners. The idea is that in future years the nigella, the grass and the biennial eryngium will self-seed into the gravel. They will also probably self-seed into the surrounding garden, providing an ever-changing note of spontaneity.

1. Any reasonable soil in full sun will suit this planting, with quite a few of the plants being happy in dry or poor soils, such as the ceanothus, anthemis and linums. The ceanothus and bupleurum may suffer in very frosty areas or if flayed by cold winter winds, although they easily cope with mild, maritime gales.

2. The ceanothus will need replacing often, approximately 8–10 years, while the anthemis might survive for only 2–3 years, though it can be propagated by division or cuttings.

3. The central pot contains one species, the *Bidens ferulifolia*, that is only half-hardy and short-lived, and one tender plant, the solanum, that needs to be brought under cover for the winter. It is possible to train this sometimes untidy and rapid-growing shrub as a standard, allowing a new shoot to replace the old central stem every other year.

[Left] *Camassia leichtlinii*

[Right] *Bupleurum fruticosum*

Bearded irises border a path at
Tintinhull, a Somerset garden
which inspired Penelope
Hobhouse when she visited while
in her twenties and which later
became her home

Penelope Hobhouse

Penelope Hobhouse is well known for her study of colour in the garden and for her involvement in many garden restorations. Alongside a successful career as a writer, she has run a garden design business, overseeing historically oriented restoration projects and creating gardens for private clients in Europe and the USA.

'Most people think I'm a traditionalist, which is not really true,' Penelope declares. 'I'm not so much interested in getting exactly the right colours next to each other as in choosing plants that are going to be happy together.' Indeed, her enthusiasms are wide ranging. She is interested in contemporary nature-inspired planting design, for example, and feels 'passionate' about unusual plants. She is 'very interested in modern architecture', which has influenced her garden designs, 'although it is difficult to say why. I love the new buildings in Chicago – seeing them from many different angles was one of the most exciting days of my life – and the Guggenheim museum in Bilbao.' Knowledge and appreciation of garden history is 'background grammar' to her designs and many of her books show her love of historical research and attention to detail.

Penelope's highest profile project is the garden designed for the late Queen Elizabeth, the Queen Mother, at Walmer Castle, Kent, UK, which like much of her design work is considered 'traditional', yet is more accurately summed up as '20th-century English'. This is the school of Gertrude Jekyll and Vita Sackville-West, where formal structures are

[Left] The 'lollipop' heads
of *Robinia pseudacacia*
'Umbraculifera' provide the
main structural element in
Penelope Hobhouse's
current garden

[Right] Masses of
butterfly-attracting
Verbena bonariensis in a
border at Walmer Castle,
Kent, in mid-summer.
Usually dotted around in
borders, the long-flowering
and drought-tolerant
perennial is rarely seen
massed in this way

balanced with an almost insouciant cottage-garden style informality, and where the creation of intimate themed spaces is a key element. Pergolas, shrubs and roses provide vertical elements and bulk, perennials fill out spaces, while hedges divide and add definition. 'Gardens,' Penelope has written, 'are about using space, they are "rooms", volumes of cubic space, which relate to their surroundings.' She considers plants to be the most important architectural elements and uses 'small trees with broad, globular or pyramidal heads' to act as '"ceilings" to enhance the room-like effects'. This is

apparent in her own walled garden in Dorset where round-headed specimens of *Robinia pseudoacacia* 'Umbraculifera' are the tallest elements.

Penelope first became interested in gardening when she was in her twenties, after visiting Tintinhull in Somerset, where she was inspired by the strong lines of the layout and was 'bowled over by the colour schemes'. Interestingly, she returned to Tintinhull in later life, living in the house as a tenant of the National Trust. In the meantime, for 12 years she lived at Hadspen House in

Somerset, where her love of gardening and garden history really took off. She worked on the neglected 3.5 hectare (9 acre) garden with Eric Smith, whose expertise in growing and selecting new perennial cultivars helped inspire her own developing plant knowledge. 'I became very interested in plants', and, she adds, 'especially shrubs' because they played an important role in the reclamation and management of the Hadspen garden, where the aim was to establish 'an overall effect of a controlled wilderness'. (The kitchen garden area has since been developed by Nori and Sandra Pope, see pages 162–167.)

Gradually though, Penelope realized that there was a danger in being too concerned simply with the aesthetics of plantings. 'If people don't consider the habitat of a plant, and look only at the picture,' she says, the planting tends to look inappropriate. She is still surprised at how many gardeners do not consider ecology when designing plantings, 'especially since Beth Chatto has set a new standard for doing this. Part of the problem,' Penelope adds, 'is that we lose sight of the importance of the soil when nearly everything is grown in containers; it is not so easy to relate plants to their conditions when they are

bought in a pot.' Indeed, instead of being depressed by the 'waterlogged clay' in her Dorset garden, she says how 'good it has been for me', in 'making me think about choosing plants that will really grow well here'. Penelope clearly loves working, both at her desk, and 'in physically gardening'; only someone who is totally committed to their craft could be so happy about a clay soil.

Designing in the USA brought Penelope face to face with many gardens that used native plants or worked with a more naturalistic aesthetic and incorporated semi-wild areas in the garden. In some projects she found herself creating plantings that had to fit into settings of natural beauty where the 20th-century English look would have been inappropriate. She also met designers who were quite militant in their desire to reject the whole English garden tradition. The vast drifts of grasses and perennials created by seminal American garden designers Wolfgang Oehme and James Van Sweden could not be more different to the hedge-defined 'rooms' of much of Penelope's work. 'I do love the Oehme Van Sweden style,' she says, 'although grasses in Britain and Europe can be more

problematic,' and has even worked with James on one project. However, Penelope is emphatic that a garden is not a natural space, for if it were truly 'natural' it would not be a garden, and no garden will look after itself. 'Wild gardening is some of the most skillful of all', she says. Her experiences led to *Natural Planting* (Pavilion, 1999), her book on the new nature-inspired plantings, interpreted as a contemporary re-working of the ideas of the late-Victorian Irish-born gardening writer William Robinson.

'Structure is so important,' Penelope says, even in wild gardens. For those who think of structure only in terms of formality, it is instructive to hear Penelope outline the various ways in which structure can be used in gardens. 'You do not need a formal garden for structure,' she says, 'some clipped yews or a single enclosing clipped hedge is all that is needed to give a garden a sense of framework. Structure,' she adds, 'can also be created by repeating groups of plants, but not necessarily symmetrically. It's very important that something repeats, even if the planting is too small to have the same thing repeated, there should be something else that hints at a particularly

prominent colour or form.' She stresses too that structure also depends upon having plenty of interesting foliage shapes, with evergreens particularly useful for supplying these. Repetition is something that is key to the naturalistic planting movement too, an element that is particularly striking at the garden of the Weihenstephan Institute, near Munich. This is one of several gardens that Penelope has visited in Germany which explore a very different, essentially naturalistic, aesthetic, and one that has made an especially strong impression on her. Long rectangular beds are planted with a wide variety of perennials, along with some shrubs and annuals, many of them part of systematically organised collections. However a strong visual effect is made through key plants being repeated, so that a remarkably strong rhythm is built up.

Italy, Penelope's greatest foreign love and the primary source of the formal tradition in Western garden history, has taught her valuable lessons: in the Italian Renaissance garden 'all is geometric, in balance and perfectly proportioned', she explains. 'There are allegorical meanings,' she says, 'which few gardens have today.' Like the Muslim concept of the garden as a spiritual oasis, 'earlier gardens had connections to philosophy and spirituality'. (She has visited Iran three times and is writing a book on Persian gardens.) She is excited by the increasing involvement of new ideas in gardening: 'Cutting edge ideas are excellent and gardens that create links with art and ideas are tremendously important, although the key thing is what impression they make when a visitor first steps inside.' To illustrate this she talks about her visit to Charles Jencks' Garden of Cosmic Possibilities in Scotland, which has become one of the best known allegorical gardens. 'I went by myself and absolutely loved it,' she says, 'although then I didn't have the faintest idea of what it was all about.'

Art and landscape have both inspired Penelope garden design work, with Monet, Turner and Claude all having, she believes, important lessons for gardeners. Landscape is important for her too, 'perhaps even more so than art in museums'. 'Ploughed fields or corn stubble have their own beauty, and I love looking out over the rolling hills of my own Dorset landscape.'

[Left] The use of box hedging to create formal patterns is a very traditional style of gardening. Here it is used to give order to a relaxed perennial planting in Penelope Hobhouse's own garden

[Previous Page] Penelope's informal style uses strongly architectural plants, shaped shrubs and gravel paths to create structure in her garden

Penelope no longer designs gardens, preferring now to concentrate on writing and on consultancy work. The latter she finds 'so much easier' than design, mainly because of the difficulties associated with keeping in touch with how gardens develop. One of the central problems of the garden designers' art is that their work is never truly finished and they are nearly always dependent upon the efforts of others for the fulfillment of their vision. Designers who walk away from their work, never returning, exert no control over how it develops; yet to continue to be involved, as Penelope prefers, assumes that the owners' vision of the garden's development is reasonably consistent with that of the designer and that they are prepared to pay for follow-up and supervisory visits. 'Owners so often mess the gardens around and it can be a problem if, for example, they get too keen, and start cramming in too many plants,' she says. 'Then there are problems of who you deal with, owners, managers, gardeners, and how long they stay in the job.'

Discussing recent developments in popular gardening culture, Penelope describes how she is a 'terrific fan of Alan Titchmarsh', the British TV garden presenter, who introduced the concept of 'make-over' gardens. She confesses that while her 'first feeling was that it was a product not a process', she gradually realized: 'Alan was introducing gardening to a whole new range of people who had never gardened before and his approach has quite revolutionized the nursery trade.' But completely

re-making a garden in a short space of time in front of the cameras is harder to take. 'Why all the rush? I don't see why it all has to be done so quickly.'

Penelope's current garden in Dorset includes an inner walled enclosure of some 40 by 40 metres, with a network of formal gravel paths that often merge with areas of gravel-covered bed. The feeling in winter is very Mediterranean, both because of the clipped box and other formal elements, but also because of the emphasis on evergreen foliage. 'I love evergreen shrubs more than anything,' she says. 'In a few years there will be nothing here but greys and greens. I'm quite happy with that, but it is not so easy to sell to other people.' In summer though, the dominance of evergreens is disguised by a variety of deciduous shrubs, perennials and grasses, some growing out over the paths to soften the garden's underlying framework, others busily seeding into the gravel. The high walls act as a shelter from the elements and from the outside world, and help to protect slightly tender species such as *Acacia pravissima* and *Euphorbia mellifera*. It is a garden that combines discipline and modesty with natural exuberance, a fitting balance for reflecting the range of interests of Penelope's garden career.

A rectangular island bed around smoke bushes

plant list

1. *Kniphofia uvaria nobilis* (10)
2. *Helianthus* 'Lemon Queen' (9)
3. *Lysimachia ciliata* 'Firecracker' (9)
4. *Hemerocallis* 'Stafford' (14)
5. *Artemisia* 'Powis Castle' (6)
6. *Cotinus* 'Grace' (2)
7. *Cephalaria gigantea* (7)
8. *Lilium* 'Enchantment' (12)
9. *Alchemilla mollis* (7)
10. *Crocosmia* 'Lucifer' (9)
11. *Eupatorium purpureum* 'Atropurpureum' (9)
12. *Coreopsis verticillata* 'Moonbeam' (9)
13. *Crocosmia* 'Lady Hamilton' (9)
14. *Monarda* 'Purple Ann' (9)
15. *Euphorbia characias* subsp. *wulfenii* (4)
16. *Hemerocallis citrina* (7)
17. *Lysimachia ephemerum* (9)
18. *Potentilla* 'William Rollison' (6)
19. *Foeniculum vulgare* 'Purpureum' (5)
20. *Helianthus* 'Beldermeir' (9)
21. *Euphorbia griffithii* 'Fireglow' (7)
22. *Artemisia ludoviciana* (5)
23. *Crocosmia* 'Star of the East' (9)

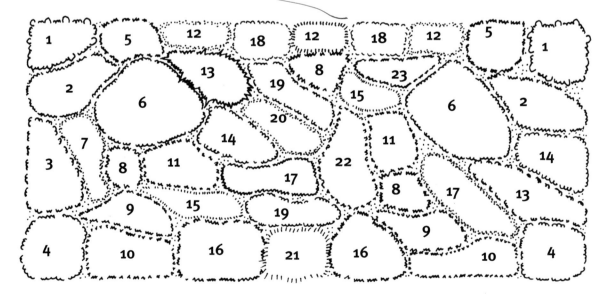

'Because I like enclosed spaces I don't design many island beds,' says Penelope, 'which means that most of the borders I design have a back.' But she concedes that island beds do have some advantages. 'You can look across them and see them from more angles than you can when a border backs on to a wall or hedge. The picture is never static.'

'I designed this particular bed with a lot of purple-bronze foliage, a colour that is not as strong as that of many of the purple-leaved plants that are often used, and that associate well with yellow flowers which are paler yellow on the north side and stronger on the sunnier side.'

A good example of the lighter purple is *Cotinus* 'Grace', a pair of which act as a pivot for the whole bed. It is a shade lighter than the more commonly seen variety 'Royal Purple'. The two cotinus plants are the only true woody shrubs in this bed, and virtually act as its skeleton; even in winter their bare twigs provide some structure.

Late winter sees a couple of *Euphorbia characias* subsp. *wulfenii* slowly begin to unfurl their yellow-green flower heads from out of their grey-leaved clumps. Penelope waxes lyrical about euphorbias, saying how she would like to collect more of them, and how valuable many are in springtime. As spring advances the purple-leaved herbaceous plants in the border begin to make their presence felt, such as *Lysimachia ciliata* 'Firecracker' and *Foeniculum vulgare* 'Purpureum'. And the silver-felted leaves of *Artemisia ludoviciana* make a dramatic contrast to the nearby purples.

In early to midsummer this planting really get into its stride with yellow-green *Alchemilla mollis* and lemon-yellow *Hemerocallis citrina*, for example. Midsummer sees two tall clumps of *Cephalaria gigantea* in flower, an unusual plant because its pale primrose-yellow flowers are a rare colour at the best of times, especially now. At a similar height of 2m (7ft), but flowering slightly later, is *Eupatorium purpureum* 'Atropurpureum', its dull pink, fluffy flower heads making up for their somewhat dirty colour by attracting hordes of butterflies. The purple monardas are another feature at this time, and also attract plenty of insects.

Helianthus 'Lemon Queen' is the star at the end of the growing season, its pale yellow flowers borne over a long period into autumn, a colour that can be a welcome relief from the strong yellows that tend to dominate at this time. In Penelope's design these perennial sunflowers are the only really tall plants at the edges of the bed. Island beds are usually structured so that the taller plants are in the centre and the shorter ones towards the outside. Placing these floriferous plants at the edge helps 'frame the picture'. Their yellow is picked up by the hot colours of the crocosmias that, with the fiery tones of the autumn colours of the cotinus, end the season on a high.

REQUIREMENTS

1. The plants in this border tolerate a wide range of soil conditions but need a sunny open position. Some of the later-flowering perennials, such as the monardas and the eupatorium, may not appreciate a prolonged period of drought. A thick mulch of wood chips or shredded plant material will help conserve moisture in the ground, and ensure that the later-flowering perennials perform well.

2. This is a very good planting for the long-term, with virtually all the species being very long-lived. The only possible exception is the monarda, that has a tendency to die out in the centre, with its new growth creating a new outer edge. In other words, the plant gradually moves, leading to possible competition with neighbouring perennials. When this happens, the monardas need to be dug up in spring and replanted.

3. The main long-term problem is caused by most of the perennials forming large clumps that may compete with each other. Some, such as *Euphorbia griffithii* 'Fireglow' and *Lysimachia ciliata* 'Firecracker', will do this faster than others, and may need to be reduced in size by division after three or four years. On light soils, the artemesia may be invasive. The cotinus may eventually become quite large and need pruning back; this can be done ruthlessly, even to ground level, without any fear of killing it.

A scented winter border in shade, with some spring and summer flowers

plant list

1. *Choisya ternata* (1)
2. *Corylopsis pauciflora* (1)
3. *Sarcococca hookeriana* var. *humilis* (10)
4. *Brunnera macrophylla* (24)
5. *Arum italicum* 'Marmoratum' (5)
6. *Euphorbia schillingii* (5)
7. *Cotoneaster lacteus* (1)
8. *Hamamelis mollis* (1)
9. *Philadelphus* 'Belle Etoile' (3)
10. *Anemone nemorosa* (25)
11. *Symphytum* × *uplandicum* 'Variegatum' (3)
12. *Helleborus* × *hybridus* (18)
13. *Garrya elliptica* 'James Roof' (18)
14. *Viburnum* × *burkwoodii* (1)
15. *Rhamnus alaternus* 'Argenteovariegata' (1)
16. *Cornus stolonifera* 'Flavirnamea' (3)
17. *Daphne odora* 'Aureo-marginata' (1)
18. *Lonicera tragophylla* (2)
19. *Hedera helix* 'Buttercup' (5)
20. *Ilex* × *altaclerensis* 'Golden King' (9)
21. *Lonicera* × *purpusii* 'Winter Beauty' (2)
22. *Hamamelis* × *intermedia* 'Jelena' (1)
23. *Ligustrum ovalifolium* 'Aureum' (1)
24. *Hydrangea petiolaris* (1)
25. *Sarcococca hookeriana* var. *digyna* (5)
26. *Philadelphus coronarius* 'Aureus' (1)

Wall

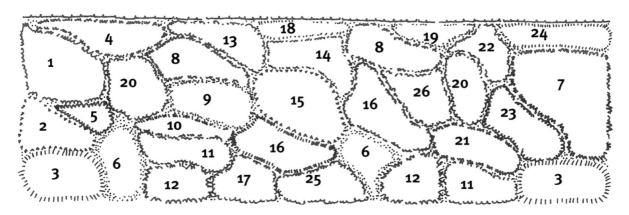

Borders that receive little sunlight, such as those which are north-facing, need shade-tolerant woodland plants if they are to succeed. These include many evergreen winter-flowering shrubs that naturally live in woodland, and that enjoy the bright conditions in winter when most of the trees have dropped their leaves.

The winter-performing shrubs in this border include two hollies (*Ilex × altaclerensis* 'Golden King') that form a golden variegated backbone to the border. Despite the name, they are female and will bear a good crop of berries in the autumn if there are male hollies in the vicinity. The border is further framed by bulky evergreens with the spring-flowering *Choisya ternata* at one end and a red-berried *Cotoneaster lacteus* at the other. The sense of framing is enhanced by the three sarcococca groups at the front; they are evergreen with sweetly scented flowers in late winter.

The two hazels (*Hamamelis*) flower in winter, and the related corylopsis a little later in spring, having curious

little blossoms with an extraordinarily sweet and far-carrying scent. The winter-flowering honeysuckle (*Lonicera × purpusii* 'Winter Beauty'), the *Garrya elliptica* 'James Roof' and *Helleborus × hybridus* also flower at this time. Winter interest is further enhanced by the variegated foliage of the centrally-placed *Rhamnus alaternus* 'Argenteovariegata', the golden-variegated *Ligustrum ovalifolium* 'Aureum' and the yellow stems of the dogwood (*Cornus stolonifera* 'Flaviramea').

As winter turns into spring, many of the perennials used in this border start into growth, and being edge-of-woodland plants in bright positions they make strong growth relatively early in the season. They include *Brunnera macrophylla* that flowers in mid-spring, *Arum italicum* 'Marmoratum' with its variegated leaves and *Symphytum × uplandicum* 'Variegatum' with broad, cream-margined leaves. Notice how the bulky, green-leaved brunnera is situated at the rear, filling space at the base of the wall and the shrubs, and how the perennials

with more showy, variegated foliage are sited
in a more prominent position at the front.

The spring also sees a steadily spreading carpet of the
delicate white flowers of *Anemone nemorosa*, a species
that can be slow initially. And, in late spring, *Viburnum* ×
burkwoodii and *Daphne odora* 'Aureo-marginata' produce
their richly scented flowers.

Towards the front of the border are two plants of
Euphorbia schillingii, Penelope's 'favourite out of all the
euphorbias'. Their elegant leaves have a central, creamy
vein while the red-flushed stems act as a foil to the greeny-
yellow flowers borne in early summer. Also flowering in
early summer is the sweetly scented *Philadelphus
coronarius* 'Aureus', a relatively compact form that has
yellow-tinged leaves which scorch easily in strong
sunlight, making it an ideal variety for this shady spot. And
on the wall at the rear are two climbers, the yellow-
flowering honeysuckle (*Lonicera tragophylla*), and the
white, self-clinging *Hydrangea petiolaris*.

[Left] *Hamamelis* × *intermedia* 'Jelena'

[Right] *Hamamelis mollis*

REQUIREMENTS

1. Being mostly woodland plants, these species benefit from a humus rich, free-draining soil that stays moist through the summer. Of all the plants used, the daphne, hamamelis and corylopsis most need these conditions; the latter two have a reputation for doing better on acid or neutral soil.

2. All the shrubs and perennials used are notably long-lived, which means this planting could last for decades. Problems of serious competition will only result if the plants are arranged too closely. Shrubs that become too large, relative to their neighbours, will need pruning to reduce their size at some stage, and some of the perennials, the symphytum especially, will need thinning out. Eventually, depending upon planting distances, the shrubs will tend to intermesh, forming a solid mass. This may be so dense that it denies space or light to the perennials. In the long-term, the diversity of this planting will therefore decrease without any intervention, but it will become lower maintenance.

A mixed shrub border in full sun

plant list

1. *Clematis* 'Bill Mackenzie'   (1)
2. *Polygonatum odoratum*
   'Variegatum'   (7)
3. *Nepeta* 'Six Hills Giant'   (10)
4. *Leptospermum* × *grandiflorum*   (1)
5. *Phlomis longifolia*   (5)
6. *Agapanthus campanulatus*   (14)
7. *Cephalaria gigantea*   (14)
8. *Salvia guaranitica* 'Blue
   Enigma'   (7)
9. *Campanula lactiflora* 'Pritchard's
   Variety'   (18)
10. *Verbascum chaixii*   (14)
11. *Abutilon vitifolium*   (1)

12. *Bupleurum fruticosum*   (1)
13. *Euphorbia longifolia*   (5)
14. *Alchemilla mollis*   (18)
15. *Verbascum pyramidatum*   (7)
16. *Baptisia australis*   (3)
17. *Lavandula angustifolia* 'Hidcote'   (2)
18. *Stauntonia hexaphylla*   (1)
19. *Salvia uliginosa*   (18)
20. *Rosa* 'Frühlingsgold'   (1)
21. *Clematis* 'Perle d'Azure'   (1)
22. *Ceanothus* 'Italian Skies'   (1)
23. *Clematis tangutica*   (1)
24. *Cytisus battandieri*   (1)
25. *Lilium* 'Golden Splendour'   (24)
26. *Euphorbia schillingii*   (5)
27. *Phlomis fruticosa*   (2)

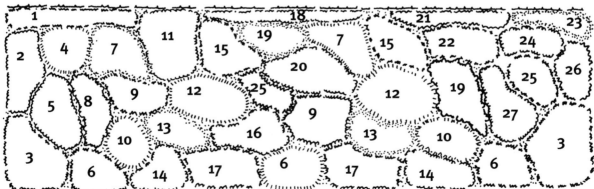

This border perhaps represents Penelope Hobouse's interests most clearly. 'It is for a fairly mild climate,' she says, and 'reflects my passion for broad-leaved evergreen shrubs, greys and greens, euphorbias and phlomis,' whose shapes, colours and textures provide structure and a particularly strong sense of continuity. The predominant colour scheme is violet-blue and yellow right through the summer, with enough evergreens to provide winter interest.

The front is framed by lavender and, at the corners, there is a foaming mass of catmint (*Nepeta* 'Six Hills Giant'). The wall at the back is planted with a variety of clematis, including two of the so-called lemon-peel ones ('Bill Mackenzie' and *C. tangutica*) that flower later than most, from mid- to late summer. In the centre is the climber *Stauntonia hexaphylla* with wonderful, scented, creamy flowers in spring and rather exotic-looking, divided leaves. There is a good mixture of plant forms here, many of the shrubs having a mound-like growth habit to contrast with the more upright habit of many of the perennials, especially the starkly upright spikes of two verbascums. 'I love the upright verbascums,' says Penelope, 'and I love them to self-seed, although this cannot be expected if a mulch is used.'

REQUIREMENTS

This border really gets going in early summer, with the pale yellow rose 'Frühlingsgold', several euphorbias, the nepetas and ever-useful *Alchemilla mollis*. Early summer also sees the flowering of the ceanothus, abutilon, pineapple-scented Moroccan broom (*Cytisus battandieri*), and the the herbaceous *Baptisia australis* with its lead-blue, pea-like flowers that are followed by attractive, near-black seed heads.

A little later in summer, the lilies flower and the shrub *Bupleurum fruticosum* has a mass of green-yellow bloom. This is another of Penelope's favourites, and is typical of the Mediterranean, evergreen shrubbery to which she is so drawn but which may be too subtle for some tastes. It forms a subtle centrepiece for this border, and provides a good foil for the stronger colours.

There are some good blues for midsummer, including agapanthus and *Campanula lactiflora*. The *Leptospermum* × *grandiflorum* also flowers about now, making a shrub (or sometimes small tree) that is somewhat tender (like the rest of its genus), although it is obviously a favourite of Penelope's. 'I think it is the hardiest leptospermum and the one most adaptable to alkaline soil. It is also the most reliable and has very good sized white flowers.' While it loves sun and needs good drainage, it must be in a position where it will never dry out.

Late summer and autumn are lit up by the exceptionally clear blue flowers of *Salvia uliginosa* and the deep blue *Salvia guaranitica* 'Blue Enigma', two of many exceptionally rich colours provided by the salvia group.

1. This border is built around plants that appreciate a mild climate. The wall provides protection, reflecting the sun's heat back on to the border, and keeps off strong winds. Interestingly, several of the evergreens, notably the bupleurum and leptospermum, tolerate strong, mild sea winds but hate cold winds. Any reasonable soil will suit the majority of the plants, but it should not be drought prone or some species will suffer. The phlomis, lavandula and ceanothus are the most drought tolerant, the *Salvia uliginosa* the least.

2. This scheme should continue to give pleasure for many years because only a few of the species used are short-lived: the verbascums are little more than biennials but nearly always self-sow, while the abutilon and ceanothus will last for 7–10 years, and the low Mediterranean shrubs – lavender and phlomis – will eventually become scraggily senescent and need replacing. Annual light pruning will help keep them tidy though, giving them a lifespan of 12–15 years. The verbascums will self-sow on most soils, scattering themselves around, that helps create a natural, spontaneous atmosphere. Only occasionally will self-seeding become a problem, but surplus seedlings are easily hoed off.

3. The clematis will benefit from annual pruning, the heaviness of which depends upon how much they need to be restricted in size. In areas that might experience a severe frost, the plant can be protected by a thick winter mulch of straw, well weighted down.

Penelope Hobhouse A mixed shrub border in full sun

A border in sun, backed by a yew hedge

plant list

1. *Thalictrum glaucum* (10)
2. *Phlox maculata* 'Alpha' (10)
3. *Geranium* 'Johnson's Blue' (12)
4. *Anaphalis margaritacea* var. *cinnamomea* (18)
5. *Kniphofia* 'Wrexham Buttercup' (10)
6. *Crambe cordifolia* (10)
7. *Clematis recta* (2)

8. *Phormium cookianum* (10)
9. *Anemone* 'Honorine Jobert' (10)
10. *Lilium regale* var. *album* (10)
11. *Euphorbia characias* subsp. *wulfenii* 'Lambrook Gold' (3)
11. *Euphorbia characias* subsp. *wulfenii* 'John Tomlinson' (3)
12. *Perovskia atriplicifolia* (24)
13. *Aster* × *frikartii* 'Mönch' (18)
14. *Galega orientalis* (10)
14. *Galega officinalis* (10)
15. *Aconitum carmichaelii* 'Arendsii' (7)
16. *Gaura lindheimerii* (16)
17. *Iris pallida* (18)
18. *Phlomis fruticosa* (1)
19. *Clematis macropetala* (2)
20. *Clerodendrum trichotomum* (1)
21. *Olearia* 'Waikariensis' (1)

Yew Hedge

Designed to provide a long summer of blues, yellows and some whites, this border is backed by a yew hedge whose dark foliage makes a splendid backdrop to most colours. It is largely herbaceous, with only three shrubby species. There is *Clerodendrum trichotomum* with white flowers in late summer, followed by its rather extraordinary turquoise berries, and the yellow flowers of *Phlomis fruticosa* and *Olearia* 'Waikariensis'. The olearia is one of the New Zealand daisy bushes and is a particular favourite of Penelope's, being covered in clusters of white daisy-like flowers in midsummer. With the phlomis it creates the evergreen, shrubby pivot of this border. Since they do not drop their dead flowers, both will need dead-heading.

Two cultivars of *Euphorbia characias* subsp. *wulfenii* start the year off in late winter, with *Iris pallida* making early growth. Late spring or early summer sees the small, mauve-blue *Clematis macropetala* at the rear in flower with the lilac-blue iris blooming a little later, followed by *Geranium* 'Johnson's Blue' that has mauve-blue flowers and a tidy, low, clump-forming habit, perfect for the front of the border. Later on there is the white and silver *Anaphalis margaritacea* var. *cinnamomea* and the contrasting architectural spikes of the yellow-flowering *Kniphofia* 'Wrexham Buttercup'. All kniphofias are excellent border plants, especially for their vertical shapes. Their foliage also has a linear quality that contrasts with other leaf shapes in the border.

There are two clumps of the dark-eyed, pink-flowering *Phlox maculata* 'Alpha' in this scheme, that help fill what Penelope describes as 'the awkward gap' in summer, before the big flush of late summer- and autumn-flowering perennials. The two big clumps of *Perovksia atriplicifolia*, with a haze of blue flowers in midsummer, fulfil the same role. *Gaura lindheimeri* is a plant that Penelope is very enthusiastic about because it has good sized white flowers on wiry, branching stems, and looks good until well into autumn. Since the stems are not that visible from a distance, the flowers appear to hover above surrounding plants like butterflies. The flowering season ends with white *Anemone* 'Honorine Jobert' and the blue *Aster × frikartii* 'Mönch'.

Most of the plants die down over winter, leaving the two evergreen shrubs and the spiky, evergreen form of *Phormium cookianum* at the front as the main source of interest. Many plants may be cut back in the autumn, but do leave the perovskias until spring because their attractive, branching stems turn an attractive bleached colour over winter.

REQUIREMENTS

1. Any reasonable soil and an open, somewhat sheltered position will suit the plants well, all of which, with the exception of the gaura, are long-lived.

2. In time, some will outgrow their alloted spaces, particularly the anemones that form very large clumps, while in a mild climate the phormium may become very large. It is difficult to reduce a phormium in size, but all the herbaceous plants are easy to divide and the shrubs can be pruned. The clerodendrum will eventually develop a tree-like habit, creating a certain amount of shade. The geranium, anemone and euphorbias (when young) are the only species that will really thrive in this situation without regular maintenance. The phlox should be divided into sections every few years, creating more new plants.

Nöel Kingsbury

In 1994 I decided to travel abroad looking at gardens. I had done some garden design in England but was very disillusioned with most of the contemporary design work. Very little seemed to be forward-looking or experimental, and the emphasis was on evoking the glories of the past, 'tradition' and 'period' being the buzzwords. Frustrated with this lack of creativity I wanted to see what was happening overseas. After visiting Brazil, the USA and Holland (where I first met Piet Oudolf), I went to Germany where I had heard of rumours of a new ecologically based and nature-inspired planting style.

So, one fine June day I found myself in Munich's Westpark, looking down on a shallow amphitheatre of planting. It included many familiar plants – with bearded irises, red valerian, mallows, ornamental grasses and alliums – but all arranged in a way that was totally new to me. Instead of being lined up in the familiar border, they were spread out with an almost field-like generosity. There were broad paths full of people on that public holiday, but also a network of narrow paths that wended their way through the plantings, giving access to all areas, although at first sight these paths were invisible. The overall effect was that a herbaceous border had been crossed with a wildflower meadow. It was overwhelming.

I have termed this style of planting the 'open-border style' because it eliminates the rigid format of the traditional English border, where plants are looked *at* against a backdrop of a fence, wall or hedge. Instead, it makes it

possible to look *over* or even *through* them. Another eye-opener to me was that very few plants were arranged in the blocks that most English-style designers used. I was used to a style that never questioned the prevailing dogma in which, at least in medium-sized or larger borders, plants were set out in multiples, creating blocks. But in this German open border the plants were blended and intermingled, giving an effect that was much more naturalistic and, I think, more subtle, complex and sophisticated.

Those with a small garden may well ask: 'What has all this got to do with me?' More than they may think, I would argue. I have always been struck by how many Dutch front gardens, never very big, are laid out with planting all the way across instead of having narrow borders edging an area of lawn. In other words, if you do not need a lawn and like growing plants, dig it up and create a meadow-like effect. American gardeners with their vast acreages of lawn have even more possibilities.

Creating these open borders requires thinking differently about how plants are used. To create a sense of a unified whole in a large area means you need to repeat plants, and this is most effectively done with those that have a dramatic appearance (for example, kniphofias and verbascums) or which have a long season of interest (many ornamental grasses). Such repetition injects a sense of rhythm and visual unity.

Such aesthetic questions are important, but the key to this approach is plant ecology. The plantings I so admired in Munich, and later in other German cities, were developed specifically for public spaces, and were meant to be low-maintenance and low input. Building on the work of Karl Foerster, the 20th-century German nurseryman and prolific writer who inspired a whole generation of designers and gardeners, the following plans create communities of plants all chosen because their ecological requirements (for water, light and nutrients, etc.) can be readily supplied by the site.

For example, the Westpark planting was an example of steppe planting, named after the grassy environment found in eastern Europe on free-draining soils. Steppe plants have to be able to survive severe winter cold and possible drought. They are not pampered and watered as are traditional English borders. And while their main flowering period is short but spectacular, many are evergreen with attractive grey foliage, giving a long season of interest.

An emphasis on plant communities is central to the German parks approach. This is not surprising because the study of natural plant communities (known as plant sociology) has played a major part in German botany. In the wild, particular plants are found together time and time again, in roughly similar conditions. Such a predictable set of plants can then be classified as a community.

Some of the most popular combinations used in the parks utilize plants found at woodland edges, a rich habitat where plants of both open and shady places can be found together. They are often native to central Europe. Other combinations, as in the steppe plantings, use species growing in similar habitats from a wide range of countries.

Ironically, the fertile, consistently moist soils favoured by traditional gardeners, are the least suitable for the open-border style. This is because weeds thrive in such resource-rich soil while perennials and ornamental grasses have a tendency to compete aggressively against each other, detracting from the look.

[Left] The steppe area in Munich's Westpark in Germany in June, with red valerian, *Centranthus ruber*, and bearded irises the dominant feature.

[Right] Yellow spires of *Verbascum nigrum* dominate a park in Ingolstadt, Bavaria in July, the product of many years self-sowing.

[Left] A border designed by the author includes multi-coloured achillea hybrids and purple *Salvia nemorosa*

[Right] In the author's own garden, late May is dominated by purple *Geranium sylvaticum* 'Birch Lilac', which has been allowed to self-sow, and *Aquilegia vulgaris*

Interestingly, in recent years I have found many of my German colleagues paying a lot of attention to the American prairie as a model of a highly attractive plant community that flourishes on very fertile soils. Experimental work has therefore started on adapting the prairie plant community to public gardens. Prairie species are already familiar to European gardeners because many have been in cultivation as border plants for more than a century. They include monardas, rudbeckias, helianthus (perennial sunflowers) asters and solidagos.

Back home, I have been experimenting with the German approach. The mild and humid climate of the west of England creates both opportunities and problems for a low-maintenance style. The combination of unpredictable, but generally high, rainfall with a long growing season means you can be more flexible about combining plants from different habitats than in mainland Europe. For example, you can combine woodland-edge species (*Geranium endressii*) with dry meadow plants (*Salvia nemorosa*), whereas these plants would be less likely to succeed together in a region where summer and winter are more distinct.

The problems are caused by the long growing season. Most ornamental perennials are winter dormant, but some of the most aggressive weeds are able to grow right through the winter, particularly the tough pasture grasses. Failure to keep such weeds in check means that the desired perennials get swamped. Consequently, in west-coast climates there has to be a greater emphasis on weed control. Plantings that are going to be low maintenance need to be based on robust weed-suppressing perennials, wood chip mulches must be used to inhibit the growth of weed seedlings, and the removal of winter weeds with a glyphosate-based weedkiller may be a necessity.

In addition to plantings for public spaces, I have been able to monitor a long-term experiment with a large, open border, using moisture-loving perennials, at Cowley Manor Hotel, Gloucestershire, UK. Despite several years of neglect while the ownership changed, it has been very successful, with relatively little weed incursion and, despite some species spreading at the expense of others, has remained very attractive. The most aggressive spreaders have included the pink *Geranium × oxonianum*

types, although some asters have been equally vigorous, including *Aster* 'Climax'. However, in a garden they can easily be controlled while in wild gardens their vigour may be welcome.

Elsewhere in Britain, there have been other experiments with naturalistic planting. Nigel Dunnett and James Hitchmough, at the landscape department at the University of Sheffield, in the UK, have been working with a number of approaches using annuals, and perennials in rough grass and coppice (ie. using a combination of perennials and shrubs, the latter being regularly cut to the ground). At Lady Farm, Somerset, UK, owner Judy Pearce and designer Mary Payne have developed a particularly spectacular steppe-style planting where kniphofias make a dramatic appearance studding a slope with their fiery flower spikes, with a wide variety of other perennials and grasses.

The most interesting adventure, though, has been at The Garden House, Devon, UK, where head gardener Keith Wiley has been working for several years with a wide variety of nature-inspired plantings, often informed by his foreign travels. The South African Karoo desert has been the idea behind a very colourful combination of annuals, alpine meadows inspired a merging of a border of perennials with wild grasses, and Crete a stone wall covered with drought-tolerant plants.

Self-sowing is a key part of the appearance of the garden at The Garden House, with plants such as *Verbena bonariensis*, a tall, wiry stemmed, long-flowering species, scattering itself around. This is one of many species which are short-lived but survive through prolific seeding. In the garden this injects a feeling of spontaneity that can never be achieved through design alone, and which is a crucial part of many of the most successful naturalistic plantings. Another key factor is the widespread use of grasses. Since they are strongly linked to wild and semi-natural places, adding a few to a scheme immediately evokes a natural feel.

Naturalistic planting schemes undoubtedly look best on a large scale, which makes them especially suited to public spaces, where sustainable and relatively low-maintenance plantings make a viable alternative to traditional rose beds

and bedding schemes. However, I believe that there is also scope for smaller-scale plantings based on the open border style. If plant height and spread is restricted to less than 30cm (1ft), there are many species that can be used to create very attractive mixtures. Creeping evergreen species with good foliage can be particularly effective if they are allowed to merge with each other, providing a background for taller plants. Varieties of sedum, acaena, cotula and thyme are ideal for this purpose, with small grassy plants, such as forms of festuca and carex, growing out of them. There is a lot of potential here, as yet largely unexplored.

I find the whole area of naturalistic planting design incredibly exciting. There is so much to learn, so many new plants to try, and so many ways of combining them. I believe that gardeners should work with people from other disciplines to realize fully what they are doing. In particular ecologists have so much to teach us about how plants function in their habitats, with major implications for horticultural practice and design. Looking across traditional boundaries is a big part of the excitement.

Miscanthus sinesis 'Silberfeder' is a large, dramatic ornamental grass for the latter part of the growing season, here growing alongside yellow *Coreopsis tripteris*. Both thrive on moist, fertile soils and can be used in low maintenance plantings as they will survive a certain amount of weed competition. The large leaves on the left is the tree *Paulownia tomentosa*, kept as a coppiced shrub

Steppe

plant list

1. *Stipa tenuissima* (17)
2. *Molinia caerulea* 'Edith Dudzus' (1)
3. *Carex comans* (4)
4. *Tulipa sprengeri* (50)
5. *Allium schoenoprasum* (2)
6. *Allium hollandicum* (15)
7. *Campanula rotundifolia* (3)

8. *Knautia macedonica* (2)
9. *Centranthus ruber* (3)
10. *Iris germanica* (10)
11. *Salvia nemorosa* 'Ostfriesland' (2)
12. *Salvia* 'Mainacht' (2)
13. *Salvia* 'Viola Klose' (2)
14. *Thymus coccineus* (3)
15. *Aster amellus* 'King George' (2)
16. *Kniphofia* 'Little Maid' (3)
17. *Nepeta* × *faassenii* (1)
18. *Origanum laevigatum* 'Rosenkuppel' (4)
19. *Perovskia atriplicifolia* (2)

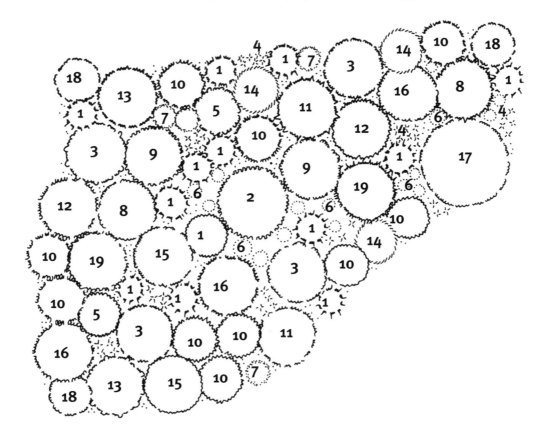

The starting point and inspiration for this hot, dry bank is the steppe, the great, dry grassland of eastern Europe. Not all the plants are actually steppe species but they are all reasonably drought resistant. They are also hardy, which makes this kind of planting more useful than Mediterranean-type schemes where the drought-resistant plants can succumb in bad winters.

Grasses, including the wispy *Stipa tenuissima* and the sedge (*Carex comans*), are the key to the naturalistic look. The former has a good nine months of interest, and the latter is evergreen, giving some winter interest. As with other dry habitats, the best season is spring and early summer, with some species continuing to provide colour until autumn. Since dry land vegetation tends to be sparse, the planting does not need to keep all the ground covered.

The bulbs could be a major feature from late winter until early summer. I have only shown two bulb species, the spring-flowering *Tulipa sprengeri* and the dramatic, early summer-flowering *Allium hollandicum*, with its ball of flowers on top of an upright, bare stem, but many more could be used.

The irises highlight the main early summer-flowering season. When choosing your favourites from the bewildering range of hybrids, make sure that they are medium-sized. They can be accompanied by salvia hybrids and the well-known *Centranthus ruber*. Later on, *Knautia macedonica* starts producing its extraordinary dark red flowers, that often carry on until late summer. *Kniphofia* 'Little Maid' flowers at the same time. While not amongst the most drought-resistant species, it has that rather exotic look that people often expect from dry plantings. Its strikingly upright form is also markedly different from that of the other plants used here. 'Little Maid' is comparatively small but in larger plantings, bigger cultivars with stronger colours could be used.

Late summer and autumn tend to be relatively sombre in dry climates. However, this combination includes an origanum, aster and perovskia that provide good colour at this time. The salvias and the nepeta will also repeat flower now if they are cut back after their main flowering in early summer. Summer rain or watering also helps promote repeat flowering.

In areas with milder winter temperatures, where the minimum rarely dives below −10°C (12°F), these plants could be combined with Mediterranean dwarf shrubs, for example species of cistus, lavender and phlomis etc. This adds a further dimension in form and more winter interest from the grey and silver foliage.

REQUIREMENTS

1. Ideal for a dry site or a thin alkaline soil, this planting is also possible on any well-drained soil, including a slope or bank.

2. Given that there are gaps between many of the plants, weed infiltration may be a problem. On flat or gently sloping sites this can be overcome by using a gravel mulch that will also help conserve moisture in the ground and provide an excellent seed bed for self-sowing species, such as the centranthus and carex. Some weeding of especially vigorous species may be necessary.

3. This is definitely a long-term planting, and any species that do die out after five years or so (possibly the centranthus and salvias) will often self-seed and create replacement plants

4. Irises tend to form large, spreading clumps after a few years, with a decline in vigour, and possible collisions with neighbouring plants. When this happens, they can be dug up when dormant and divided, with some of the sections being replanted.

5. The bearded irises (*Iris germanica*) need to have their roots exposed to the sun in temperate climates. Also, leave gaps for bulbs, particularly those that, like species tulips, need to get a good summer baking if they are to flower again next year.

[Left] *Tulipa sprengeri*

[Right] *Nepeta* x *faassenii,*

A low maintenance, naturalistic planting

plant list

1.	*Alchemilla mollis*	(6)
2.	*Anemone* × *hybrida* 'Honorine Jobert'	(3)
3.	*Aster divaricatus*	(10)
4.	*Aster laevis* 'Climax'	(1)
5.	*Aster lateriflorus* 'Lady in Black'	(2)
6.	*Brunnera macrophylla*	(2)
7.	*Calamagrostis* × *acutifolia* 'Karl Foerster'	(2)
8.	*Carex comans*	(6)
9.	*Eupatorium rugosum* 'Braunlaub'	(7)
10.	*Euphorbia palustris*	(1)
11.	*Geranium* × *oxonianum* 'Claridge Druce'	(3)
12.	*Geranium endressii*	(3)
13.	*Geranium* 'Johnson's Blue'	(4)
14.	*Geranium* 'Spinners'	(3)
15.	*Geranium versicolor*	(7)
16.	*Geranium* × *oxonianum* 'Wargrave Pink'	(2)
17.	*Luzula sylvatica* 'Marginata'	(9)
18.	*Persicaria amplexicaulis*	(4)
19.	*Persicaria bistorta* 'Superba'	(4)
20.	*Rudbeckia fulgida*	(9)
21.	*Vinca major*	(8)
22.	*Galanthus nivalis*	(50)
23.	*Narcissus* 'Liberty Bells'	(50)

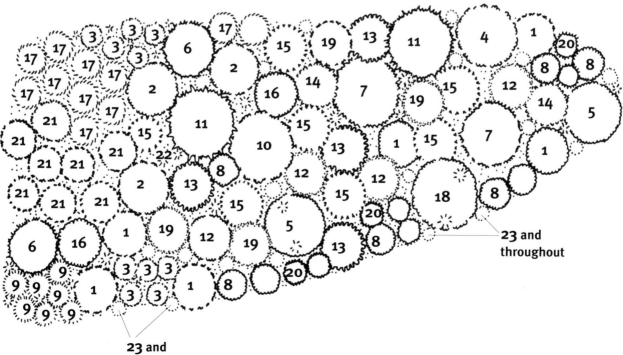

23 and throughout

23 and throughout

This design is intended for a site (for example, a slope) that is difficult to maintain. Instead of using grass that would have to be mown, or shrubs that can look dull for much of the year, use robust perennials that are good at looking after themselves and which effectively smother weeds.

Another feature is the way in which different plant combinations are used as the distance from the tree increases. The area around the base of the tree is shady and dry, where only the most robust species will grow. They include the glossy evergreen *Luzula sylvatica* 'Marginata', that eventually forms tight mats, and the evergreen periwinkle (*Vinca major*), that has blue flowers in spring.

Where light and soil moisture levels begin to increase away from the tree, there are two white, late summer-flowering perennials, *Eupatorium rugosum* 'Braunlaub'

and *Aster divaricatus*. These plants are all grouped together to ensure that they form solid clumps with time, otherwise they might compete with each other, which can lead to one variety smothering the others.

In the lighter shade under the outer canopy of the tree are four key plants with a variety of geraniums. The four are *Brunnera macrophylla,* with blue flowers in spring and large, weed-smothering leaves, *Anemone × hybrida* 'Honorine Jobert', with pure white flowers in late summer and autumn, *Persicaria bistorta* 'Superba', with pink flower spikes in late spring, and the low-growing, lime-green *Alchemilla mollis*, with lime green flowers.

The pink geraniums provide the backbone of this planting. They include *Geranium × oxonianum* 'Claridge Druce', *G. endressii*, *G. × oxonianum* 'Wargrave pink' and *G. versicolor*. They are very useful as weed-smothering ground-cover, especially for west coast gardens where a long growing season sees plenty of evergreen weeds, such as grasses and creeping buttercup. The geraniums' semi-evergreen nature allows them to compete against such weeds, and their repeat-flowering habit makes them very decorative. Two of the slightly less vigorous blue geraniums ('Johnson's Blue' and 'Spinners') are included for contrast.

The other elements in the planting fall into two categories, the taller upright plants and the front of border plants. The former provide variation in height, structural interest and give colour at times when the geraniums are not at their best. The latter provide a tidy edge to the planting on the lower side, which is the most visible one in this garden.

The main structural plant among the tall uprights is *Calamagrostis* × *acutiflora* 'Karl Foerster', its bolt upright flower and seed heads making a striking feature from early summer to late winter. *Euphorbia palustris* provides a mound of yellow-green flowers in spring and some good autumn colour, while *Persicaria amplexicaulis* develops into a similar shape with masses of deep pinky-red spikes in the latter part of the season. Finally there are two asters, the very vigorous, clump-forming, purple-blue *A. laevis* 'Climax' and *A. lateriflorus* 'Lady in Black' that, by late summer, forms an almost shrub-like shape, covered in attractive dark foliage, before smothering itself with tiny, pale pink flowers in autumn.

The front of border plants include a bronze evergreen sedge (*Carex comans*), and the dark-eyed yellow *Rudbeckia fulgida* that flowers during the autumn. Both are short plants that can always be relied upon to look tidy.

The bare ground of perennial-based plantings can be unattractive in spring, but bulbs make all the difference. Here snowdrops (*Galanthus nivalis*) are scattered in clumps, with a spring-flowering daffodil (*Narcissus* 'Liberty Bells'). Smaller daffodils are better than larger ones because the somewhat untidy leaves left after flowering are less noticeable.

REQUIREMENTS

1. Any reasonable soil in good sunlight is suitable for this design, but not where there is too much tree shade. Most of the species used are tolerant of a wide range of conditions, with only prolonged drought, waterlogging or very poor soil being unsuitable. Being robust growers, no soil preparation is generally required, apart from weeding.

2. This is a low-maintenance scheme requiring only one session of work a year after the first year. With the exception of the vinca and luzula, all the plants produce a substantial quantity of dead growth at the end of the season, which should be cut off and composted. The resulting compost can be applied as a mulch the year after.

3. Although the plant selection should suppress weeds quite effectively, there may sometimes be a problem (largely from grasses) in the late winter to mid-spring period. Given the slope, the best way to deal with the weeds is to use a glyphosate-based weed killer immediately after cutting back, carefully 'spot-spraying' the weeds.

4. In the long-term, there will be quite a bit of jockeying for position by these mostly vigorous plants. The only plants likely to suffer adversely are the smaller species at the front, the carex and rudbeckia. Plants impinging on them can be dug up and divided to limit their size and spread.

A prairie-style planting

plant list

1. *Aster cordifolius* 'Little Carlow'	(4)	9. *Helianthus* 'Lemon Queen'	(10)
2. *Aster laevis* 'Arcturus'	(2)	10. *Helianthus* 'Sheila's Sunshine'	(5)
3. *Aster turbinellus*	(3)	11. *Lysimachia ciliata* 'Firecracker'	(3)
4. *Aster umbellatus*	(2)	12. *Miscanthus sinensis* 'Rotsilber'	(1)
5. *Eupatorium fistulosum*	(4)	13. *Miscanthus sinensis* 'Silberfeder'	(1)
6. *Geranium phaeum* 'Lily Lovell'	(6)	14. *Molinia caerulea* 'Transparent'	(3)
7. *Geranium psilostemon*	(3)	15. *Monarda fistulosa*	(9)
8. *Geranium sylvaticum* 'Birch Lilac'	(10)	16. *Rudbeckia* 'Juligold'	(3)
		17. *Solidago rugosa* 'Feuerwerke'	(3)
		18. *Vernonia crinita*	(3)
		19. *Veronica longifolia*	(3)
		20. *Veronicastrum virginicum*	(3)
		21. *Ajuga reptans* 'Caitlin's Giant'	(2)
		22. *Narcissus* 'February Gold'	(50)

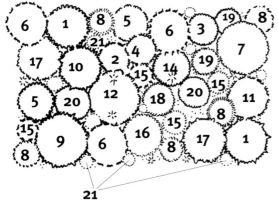

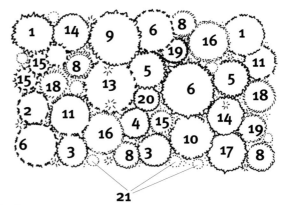

22 planted throughout

The North American prairie once covered a vast area with an incredibly rich plant community, a relatively limited number of grasses and a large number of tall, flowering herbaceous plants. Now almost entirely destroyed to make way for agriculture and urban development, remnants of the prairie have become an inspiration for contemporary naturalistic plantings.

This planting combines North American late-flowering prairie perennials with some lower-growing and earlier-flowering Eurasian species for a longer season of interest,

as well as some Eurasian grasses. The plan is designed for a site that fronts a lawn and backs onto decking, with a boardwalk connecting the two. The boardwalk is an invitation into the scheme, and provides an intimate sight of the planting. 'Into' really is the right word because the late-flowering varieties used are from 1.8–3.5m (5ft–11ft) high.

Narcissus 'February Gold' has been used to provide spring interest with the dark-leaved *Ajuga reptans* 'Caitlin's Giant'. Small narcissi and other dwarf bulbs are a good way of making later-flowering perennial plantings

interesting in spring and will be dormant by the time the perennials start to shade the ground. The evergreen ajuga provides winter interest and blue flowers in spring; it is one of the few creeping perennials that seems able to survive in the dense shade cast by the taller plants. It will eventually form sparse ground cover.

Late spring sees the deep mauve *Geranium sylvaticum* 'Birch Lilac' in flower, with emerging clumps of dark leaved *Lysimachia ciliata* 'Firecracker' and dark blue *Geranium phaeum* 'Lily Lovell'. By early summer the magenta *Geranium psilostemon* and pale blue *Veronica longifolia* and *Veronicastrum virginicum* will be making a striking combination, before the flowering of *Monarda fistulosa* kicks off the real prairie season.

The monarda has pale violet flowers but any of its hybrids, in shades of red, pink and mauve, could be used instead. From late summer until the first hard frosts, the dominant theme is yellow and blue-violet. Golden yellows will be provided by *Rudbeckia* 'Juligold' and *Solidago rugosa* 'Feuerwerke', the pale, almost primrose-yellows by

Helianthus 'Lemon Queen' and *H*. 'Sheila's Sunshine', and blue/violets by *Aster cordifolius* 'Little Carlow', *A. laevis* 'Arcturus' and *A. turbinellus*. At the very end of the season, *Vernonia crinita* contributes its distinctive red-tinged violet flowers. Also flowering now is the creamy *Aster umbellatus* and the flesh-pink *Eupatorium fistulosum* . All these late perennials are excellent butterfly-attracting plants.

A genuine prairie planting is dominated by grasses (prairie is nearly always made using a seed mix of grasses and perennials, but it can also be evoked using large grasses and perennials from a variety of different areas which must be tall and late flowering). However, here grasses are used as an additional decorative element, their winter appearance being especially valuable. Though not strictly speaking prairie grasses, they are reliable and easily available. The miscanthus cultivars are the main winter feature, but some of the other perennials have strong enough stems to withstand the winter, and can appear quite attractive. Their seed heads are potentially a good food source for birds.

[Left] Golden-yellow
Solidago rugosa
dominates this autumnal
planting of perennials.
Pale yellow *Helianthus*
'Lemon Queen' is
to the left

REQUIREMENTS

1. A site in full sun is important for this planting, with a soil that is reasonably fertile and moisture-retaining but not waterlogged.

2. The only maintenance, apart from early season weeding, is the annual cutting back of dead stems – which needs to be completed in late winter before the bulbs start to emerge. There will be plenty of dead growth for composting, but if it is going to overwhelm a modest compost heap, shred it. Then scatter the remains over the soil as a mulch to recycle nutrients.

3. Many prairie plants do not start to grow until late spring, which might mean that in regions with mild winters and a long growing season, the bare soil surface becomes a seedbed for weeds. The danger is they might get established before the bulk of the plants start to grow. This can be largely prevented by using a 3–5cm (1½–2in) deep woodchip mulch between the plants.

A glyphosate-based weedkiller can be used to kill any surviving weeds by spot-spraying them, preferably just after cutting back the perennials. Or they can be dug out by hand, but take care not to mix the mulch and the soil, ruining the effect of the former.

4. All plants here, with the exception of the monarda, form long-lived, solid clumps. However the monarda will tend to send out 'runners', resulting in the plant re-locating itself. If the border eventually becomes somewhat crowded, dig up the plant clumps and reduce them by division, using the excess sections elsewhere in the garden.

An exotic border

plant list

1. Acanthus mollis	(1)
2. Aralia racemosa	(1)
3. Bergenia cordifolia	(9)
4. Crocosmia 'Lucifer'	(2)
5. Helleborus argutifolius	(2)
6. Hosta sieboldiana 'Elegans'	(4)
7. Ligularia stenocephala 'The Rocket'	(1)
8. Ligularia dentata	(1)
9. Petasites japonicus 'Giganteus'	(1)
10. Asplenium scolopendrium	(5)
11. Polystichum setiferum	(2)

12. Indocalamus tesselatus	(1)
13. Luzula sylvatica 'Marginata'	(5)
14. Miscanthus floridulus	(1)
15. Euphorbia mellifera	(1)
16. Fatsia japonica	(1)
17. Musa basjoo	(1)
18. Paulownia tomentosa	(1)
19. Salix magnifica	(1)
20. Trachycarpus fortunei	(1)
21. Viburnum davidii	(2)
22. Aristolochia macrophylla	(1)
23. Clematis armandii	(1)

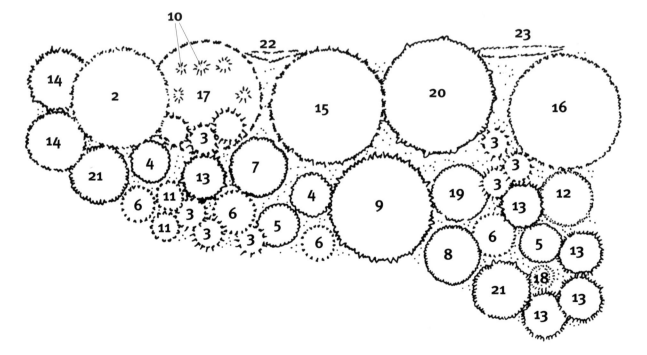

This border, designed for a south- or west-facing corner between two sheltering walls, brings together a variety of hardy plants with foliage that is luxuriant enough to convince most that they might be in the tropics. One tender species, the banana (*Musa basjoo*), is included, and is worth all efforts to protect it over winter for its spectacularly exotic appearance.

Since many of the best hardy exotica are big plants, space is needed. However, in some cases it is possible to restrict their size by pruning and other techniques. To compensate, I have tried to include plenty of smaller and more common, usually herbaceous, plants with lush foliage. When used in combination they can look quite exotic. They are also able to fill smaller spaces and act as ground cover.

The scene is set by the bamboo with its particularly broad, tropical-looking leaves and the hardy palm (*Trachycarpus*). During winter, when the bamboo has been wrapped up against the cold, the evergreen fatsia and the rounded shrub *Euphorbia mellifera* will still be here to create the right impression. A number of the smaller plants are also evergreen. They include the bergenia, hellebore and luzula. *Luzula sylvatica* is a quite exceptional plant, and with its broad leaves looks very exotic and makes effective ground cover in difficult, dry shade. The evergreen hart's tongue fern (*Asplenium scolopendrium*) is very tolerant of deep shade and can be spectacular *en masse*.

Midsummer to autumn is the best period for this border, with the ligularias flowering and the almost sugar cane-like giant grass, *Miscanthus floridulus*, reaching its maximum height of 3m (10ft). The deciduous shrubs (the paulownia and salix) will also be at their best. I say shrubs, but these two are naturally small trees. Here, however, they are kept shorter by pollarding and coppicing. These traditional techniques involve cutting back very hard to a point either well above ground level (pollarding) or close to ground level (coppicing). Not only do they keep large plants within bounds, but annual pruning results in dramatically larger-than-normal leaves. In fact visitors to my garden ask more about these plants than any other.

REQUIREMENTS

1. A site sheltered from strong winds is essential because the large leaves easily get damaged. Protection from severe frosts is not so vital, except for the euphorbia and bamboo. A fertile soil that stays reasonably moist in summer is important, especially for the ligularia and hosta.

2. The pruning of the salix and the paulownia has been mentioned. After coppicing there will be 2m (6ft) and more of growth. Pollard the paulownia at about 2m (6ft) above ground level and it will make its annual growth on top of this, creating a more tree-like effect than with the coppiced plants, while creating space to grow herbaceous plants below.

3. The giant-leaved petasites is spectacular, but especially on moist soils is dangerously invasive. However, it can be kept within bounds if planted within a barrier of heavy-duty plastic sheeting, buried vertically to a depth of 30cm (1ft). The same technique can also be used to keep the bamboo from spreading.

[Left] *Crocosmia*
'Lucifer'

[Centre] *Asplenium
scolopendrium*

[Right] *Trachycarpus
fortunei*

4. *Musa basjoo* will need protection in most gardens, particularly in the early years. The roots will survive at least –10°C [12F], but the best results are gained if the less hardy stems are protected. Wrap them in sheets of bubble-plastic, secured by wire or string, over winter. Eventually the plant will flower, bear little inedible bananas and then die, but not before producing several daughter stems, building up a substantial clump.

5. Given these management techniques this border should look good for many years. Eventually some of the perennials and ground-cover plants will become too large and compete for space, but they can easily be thinned out.

The interplay between plant
forms is the basis of Piet Oudolf's
work. In his garden in Holland in
the late summer are closely
planted groups of red *Persicaria
amplexlcaulis*, pink *Eupatorium
purpureum*, yellow *Foeniculum
vulgare*, pink *Verbena hastata*
'Rosea', blue-grey *Eryngium
giganteum*, the grass *Stipa
calamagrostis* and a pink
monarda variety

Piet Oudolf

The Dutch designer, Piet Oudolf, has become one of the
most enthusiastically received and talked about designers
today. I believe this is largely because he has achieved the
harmonious balancing of geometric structure and
seemingly unrestrained natural growth that many find so
inherently satisfying. Much of his work really is doing
something new: he uses new plants and new forms, with
a distinctly contemporary take on old themes.

The debate between the formal and informal in gardening
is one of the most enduring in garden design history. At
times, though, it has been not just a source of discord but
of important, creative energy. The relationship between
the two has tended to be dialectical, and the evolution of
the 20th-century English style, the product of Vita
Sackville-West, Gertrude Jekyll and others, has achieved
its popularity and status because it accomplished some
sort of reconciliation in this formal versus informal debate.

Strong formal structure in the form of hedges, *allées* and
geometry filled with informal burgeoning vegetation such
as herbaceous borders, shrubs, roses and exuberant
climbers give us the carefree sense of the idealized, rose-
bedecked cottage garden and the clarity and definition of
classical order. Piet Oudolf is doing the same, but in a
strikingly contemporary way.

After a career designing gardens in the Netherlands,
Piet has now gone international. With his colleague,
Arne Maynard, he won the Best Show Garden Award at

the Chelsea Flower Show, 2000, and with landscape architect Kathryn Gustafson he has designed a planting scheme for the lakeside Millennium Park complex, in Chicago, USA. He now combines working on larger public projects with private gardens.

Piet started training as a landscape gardener at age of 25. His first influence was inevitably Mien Ruys, the Bauhaus-trained designer whose architectural and modernist garden style dominated Dutch design for much of the 20th century, but who was actually very passionate about plants. 'She was everywhere, the only garden designer in Holland who was talking about plants and plantings while the others just talked about design,' Piet says. 'But by copying her, everyone clichéd what she did and her inventions lost their meaning.'

Piet's own passion for plants received a boost when he first came to England in 1977 and visited Alan Bloom's Dell Garden, in Norfolk, and Hidcote, in Gloucestershire, among other places. 'I loved the atmosphere of these gardens, the kind of dreamland, and the plants I had never seen,' he says.

At the start of his career Piet had been working in the densely populated western part of Holland. But, in 1982, he and his family moved to the more sparsely populated eastern province of Gelderland, and spent several years converting an old farmhouse in Hummelo. They also laid the groundwork for a nursery (run by his wife, Anja).

Piet was increasingly frustrated at not being able to obtain the plants he wanted for his designs, and decided to provide his own.

A key part of the next few years was spent finding these plants. In England, the Beth Chatto Nursery, in Essex, had plenty to offer, 'besides inspiring me,' he says, 'by the way that she ran the nursery... in fact she gave us the idea of setting up the nursery in the first place.' From here and elsewhere the Oudolfs bought geraniums, hellebores and lavateras, etc. German nurseries were also a valuable source of plants, in particular that of Ernst Pagels, in Ost Friesland, just across the border. Pagels had been a student of the highly influential nurseryman and writer Karl Foerster, whom Piet describes as 'my hero for his unconventional way of looking at plants'.

Piet and Anja also travelled in the Balkans collecting plants, a region especially rich in plant life, finding some particularly fine hellebores in Bosnia-Hercegovina just before the war broke out. There were as yet few customers at their nursery, Piet had temporarily stopped doing design work, and the only income was from Anja selling grasses and cut flowers to local florists. But the nursery soon took off and, in Britain, Piet was frequently known as the 'nurseryman who designs gardens' instead of the designer who had set up his own nursery.

Besides finding plants of wild origin, Piet has done a lot of work on plant selection, concentrating particularly on

asters, astrantias, monardas and sanguisorbas. Plant selection is a classic example of Dutch co-operation because Piet pays a local farmer to trial plants for him, so that he can later make a selection of the best, leaving the remainder to be ploughed in at the end of the season. Thorough and ruthless plant selection is essential. 'I need only the best,' he says.

Whereas Piet's earlier, pre-Hummelo work was strongly architectural, his later work has focused on a dramatic use of perennials, in conjunction with and counter-pointed by distinctly modern structural features.

He also emphasises that perennials have a distinct, unique structure of their own. Although colour combinations are often striking, it is, he says 'the perennials' structure that is the most important aspect in designing with them'. Plants are arranged according to the shape of their flower heads, or the overall shape of the plant. Much use is made of grasses and other plants that gardeners have previously tended to ignore, such as astrantias, sanguisorbas and umbellifers (members of the *Apiaceae* or cow-parsley family). Whatever their distinct colours, their primary appeal to Piet lies in their form and shape.

The key to understanding his exuberant combinations of perennials lies in appreciating his balance of plant structures. Piet tends to divide his perennials into categories: spires (narrow upright stems, such as digitalis), umbels (flattish, plate-like flower heads, such as achillea), buttons (scabious), and balls (alliums). These shapes are then combined to create contrasts with each other, starting with the largest and most strongly structural plants, which are often the grasses, or large perennials, such as *Eupatorium purpureum*.

He also believes that there is an important role for species with a much softer visual texture (for example, many of the grasses), or plants he describes as having 'transparency'. They include *Verbena bonariensis* and the grass *Stipa gigantea* which, though large, are nearly all stem, making it possible to see through them to the plants behind. He also likes what he calls 'filler plants'. They include the hardy geraniums that, while lacking structure, contribute flower colour, especially in the early part of the summer, before the more structural perennials have got into their stride.

At Bury Court Piet Oudolf has created a series of borders within the framework of an old farmyard. A stylized meadow of *Deschampsia cespitosa* 'Goldtau', on the right, provides a dramatic centrepiece

[Left] Mounds of *Origanum laevigatum* 'Herrenhausen', Sedum hybrid 'Munstead Red', *Astilbe chinensis* var. *taquetii* 'Purpurlanze' and monarda

[Right] The 'Dream park' at Enköping in Sweden, where large clumps of perennials, such as *Aconogonon* 'Johanneswolke', are used in a series of sinuous borders

In winter he likes the dead remains of the perennials to be left standing for as long as possible because he believes that this is when structure really counts. He is only partly joking when he says that 'a plant is only worth growing if it looks good when it is dead.' A meticulous photographer of his work, he was one of the first to appreciate the almost monochrome beauty of dead perennials in the winter frost and fog. The sharply defined seed heads of echinacea, sanguisorba, monarda and phlomis stand out in some of his designs against the indistinct forms of grass foliage or blackened eupatorium leaves. Everything looks like it ought to be familiar, but shorn of colour and petals, it can be very difficult to identify individual plants.

If all of this suggests that colour is not important, that is not true. Piet especially seems to like the mysterious dark red of *Astrantia* 'Hadspen Blood', *A. major* 'Claret' and *Cirsium rivulare* 'Atropurpureum'. But despite saying 'I am not a colour gardener' there is no doubt that Piet, at least subconsciously, is very good at creating effective colour combinations, often using strong pastels.

Piet's place in the history of garden and landscape design puts him firmly in the movement that seeks to bring back the wild and natural into the human habitat. 'My biggest inspiration is nature, not copying it but capturing the emotion,' he says. 'What I try to do is create an image of nature.' This can be particularly appreciated in late summer or autumn, when borders in his designs can almost overwhelm the onlooker with huge perennials and grasses. 'It is good to feel awe in front of plants,' he adds.

The partnership of James Van Sweden and Wolfgang Oehme in the USA is also part of this natural movement, and has been taken up by many designers in Germany.

But do not forget the other side to the Oudolf garden, which is formality. Not the clichéd formality of the classical European garden, with its right angles and straight lines, but something more contemporary and much more daring. Piet's own garden is the best place to understand this aspect of his work.

The first part of his garden features a strong diagonal path, the second a central axial one. Unlike the central axes of classical formality, with which other axes or features meet at right angles, this one has a staggered row of yew columns to either side, and runs through two asymmetric elliptical beds, filled with low ground-cover plants. It is an example of zig-zag symmetry, encouraging the viewer to look from side to side instead of ahead.

Whereas classical formality, with its dependence on right angles, tends to get to the focal points too quickly, thus being inappropriate for smaller spaces, Piet's approach makes the viewer slow down and appreciate what is on both sides. It is an effect that the art historian and gardener Sir Roy Strong describes as 'wonky baroque'.

Piet's first commission in Britain, the garden at Bury Court in Hampshire, is centred around a large area of lawn, and the diagonal thrust of its main path leads to a view over the surrounding countryside. Extensive borders of perennials and further paths entice the visitor away on either side and on to Piet's first gravel bed planting, with some wonderfully spiky eryngiums. This is a good place to appreciate a particularly characteristic Oudolf feature, the use of formal block planting.

Whereas the 20th-century English style used clipped trees essentially as a skeleton, turning them into hedges or regularly spaced geometric shapes, Piet's technique is to use them, and other formal features, to create static blocks of planting. They become an alternative to the much more dynamic and naturalistic perennial borders. Two examples at Bury Court include abstract shapes of box and a circular steel framework, like the outline of a drum, that is gradually being filled with *Cornus mas*, which is being trained up like a hedge.

Increasingly, Piet is being asked to create public plantings. Drömparken (Dream Park) in Enköping, Sweden, was the first large park he worked on, followed by extensive plantings at the Pensthorpe Waterfowl Trust at Fakenham, Norfolk, UK. In both, informal drifts of perennials are combined in large beds between gently winding paths, with no formal elements. His more recent commission at the Royal Horticultural Society's Garden, Surrey, UK, has seen him go in a completely new direction, dividing a very large double border into a series of rigid diagonal strips, each about 2m (6ft) wide, and composed of a mixture of three or four perennial varieties.

A corner planting for summer

plant list

1. *Achillea* 'Summerwine'	(2)
2. *Deschampsia cespitosa* 'Goldtau'	(1)
3. *Geranium* × *oxonianum* 'Rose Clair'	(3)
4. *Geranium* 'Sirak'	(3)
5. *Sedum* 'Bertram Anderson'	(4)
6. *Eryngium alpinum* 'Blue Star'	(2)
7. *Lythrum salicaria* 'Blush'	(4)
8. *Baptisia australis*	(2)
9. *Veronica spicata* 'Erika'	(5)
10. *Sidalcea* 'Elsie Heugh'	(4)
11. *Knautia macedonica*	(5)
12. *Sesleria autumnalis*	(1)
13. *Stachys monieri* 'Hummelo'	(5)
14. *Iris sibirica* 'Light Blue'	(4)
15. *Salvia* 'Mainacht'	(2)
16. *Geum rivale* 'Leonard'	(5)
17. *Liatris spicata*	(6)
18. *Monarda* 'Scorpion'	(1)
19. *Achillea* 'Hella Glashof'	(2)
20. *Kalimeris incisa*	(3)
21. *Astrantia major* 'Claret'	(5)
22. *Aconitum* 'Newry Blue'	(4)
23. *Briza media* 'Limouzi'	(3)
24. *Papaver orientale* 'Karine'	(2)

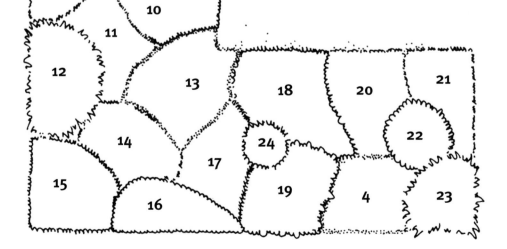

Baptisia australis

This border is designed to fit into a perpendicular space, perhaps around the corner of a house. Being highly visible it is vital that plants provide a long season of interest and continue to look, at the very least, acceptable after flowering. The design combines summer interest with some extra winter value.

The early to midsummer period sees the large pale pink flowers of the Oriental poppy (*Papaver orientale* 'Karine') with pale pink *Geranium* × *oxonianum* 'Rose Clair', the 1m (3ft) high reddish-pink *Veronica spicata* 'Erika', deep blue *Salvia* 'Mainacht' and *Iris sibirica* 'Light Blue'. A little later the achilleas start to flower, and include the deep wine-red 'Summerwine' and pale yellow 'Hella Glashof'.

During midsummer two upright perennials, the pale pink *Lythrum salicaria* 'Blush' and pale pink *Sidalcea* 'Elsie Heugh' take over, complemented by the steely grey-blue of *Baptisia australis* and the vivid violet of *Monarda* 'Scorpion'. The red-flowering *Sedum* 'Bertram Anderson' is the last to begin flowering, in late summer or early autumn, although the dark purple of its leaves has been a feature since spring.

Many of the plants selected have distinctive flower head shapes that continue to look strong well after the flowers have died. *Liatris spicata*, *Aconitum* 'Newry Blue' and *Veronica spicata* 'Erika' have distinctive spires, while *Salvia* 'Mainacht' has a more compact habit, with its masses of small, spike-like heads. Even in winter some species continue to look distinctive.

REQUIREMENTS

1. Full sun and free-draining fertile soil that can be relied upon never to dry out seriously is needed for this scheme to thrive. Fertility can be maintained by an annual (or biennial) spreading of compost, or well-rotted manure, over the soil in winter. Alternatively, shredded plant remains can be used as a winter mulch.

2. While the plants have been selected for their long period of interest, some mid-season tidying up or dead-heading may be necessary. The astrantia's dead flowers are definitely untidy looking, and the *Geranium* × *oxonianum* 'Rose Clair' has a habit of collapsing after flowering, necessitating a hard cut-back, but it will soon regrow to flower again in late summer. The rest will remain relatively tidy.

Come the autumn, how much and when to cut back is up to you. Many gardeners prefer to cut back dead plants selectively, removing the remains only of those that are definitely untidy, leaving those that have some structure and interest. But all should be cut back by late winter to avoid damaging any emerging bulbs.

This plant selection illustrates how the different growths of perennials have implications for the gardener. Some, eg.the lythrum, stay as a tight clump, the pale yellow *Geum rivale* 'Leonard's Variety' forms a tight, low clump that spreads outwards only slowly, while others, eg. the geraniums, spread more rapidly and might need digging up and dividing every few years to keep them in check.

The monarda is rather a special case because it dies out in the centre but new growth radiates outwards, necessitating occasional replanting of the wandering shoots in spring. Some of the species here may self-sow, notably the astrantia and the salvia, but there is only likely to be a problem with excessive seeding on lighter soils.

3. All the plants are long-lived, with the exception of the achilleas that are both relatively short-lived and very sensitive to winter damp. They can be kept going by lifting and dividing them every other autumn, replanting the younger shoots and discarding the old, woody material.

[Left] *Veronica spicata* 'Erika'

[Centre] *Sidalcea* 'Elsie Heugh'

[Right] *Astrantia major* 'Claret'

A circular planting for summer, with winter interest

plant list

1. *Calamintha nepeta* subsp. *nepeta* (2)
2. *Selinum wallichianum* (2)
3. *Aster ericoides* 'Blue Star' (2)
4. *Sedum* 'Matrona' (4)
5. *Perovskia atriplicifolia* 'Blue Spire' (3)
6. *Molinia caerulea* subsp. *caerulea* 'Moorhexe' (2)
7. *Monarda* 'Scorpion' (2)
8. *Eupatorium purpureum* subsp. *maculatum*
   'Atropurpureum' (1)
9. *Foeniculum vulgare* 'Giant Bronze' (4)
10. *Liatris spicata* (6)
11. *Echinacea purpurea* 'Rubinglow' (3)
12. *Veronicastrum virginica* 'Fascination' (3)
13. *Achillea* 'Credo' (3)
14. *Scabiosa japonica* var. *alpina* (4)
15. *Schizachyrium scoparium* 'The Blues' (2)
16. *Stachys monieri* 'Hummelo' (5)
17. *Miscanthus sinensis* 'Malepartus' (1)
18. *Helenium* 'Rubinzwerg' (5)
19. *Origanum* 'Rosenkuppel' (2)
20. *Nepeta racemosa* 'Walker's Low' (2)
21. *Veronicastrum virginica* 'Temptation' (3)
22. *Phlox paniculata* 'Rosa Pastell' (5)
23. *Cimicifuga simplex* 'Pritchard's Giant' (2)
24. *Limonium latifolium* (1)

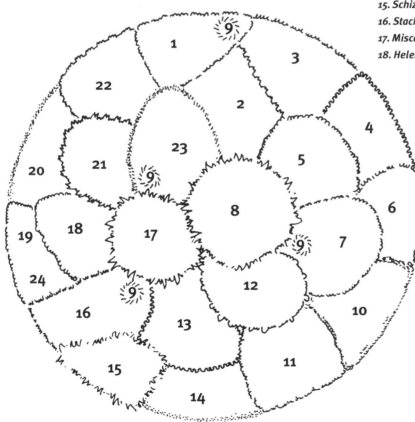

Looking its best primarily in late summer, this planting should continue to offer interest until early winter. Its overall design reflects that of the traditional island bed, with the tallest plants in the centre and the shortest on the outside. Needing good light, it makes a magnificent planting for a large lawn or other flat area where there is nothing else of comparable height nearby. The flower colours are essentially blue/violet and pink.

Flowering starts in early summer with the lavender-coloured catmint (*Nepeta racemosa* 'Walker's Low'), lilac *Stachys monieri* 'Hummelo', sulphur-yellow *Achillea* 'Credo' and the upright blue spires of *Veronicastrum virginicum*.

Most of the other species will flower in mid- to late summer, with extra autumn flowers from the pale pink *Sedum* 'Matrona' and the *Aster ericoides* 'Blue Star'

151

Height is a key element. In early summer, there is little over 40cm (16in) high, but later the 1.5m (4ft) spires of the veronica and the dark bronze heads of the fennel (*Foeniculum vulgare* 'Giant Bronze') make a strong impact. By late summer the taller species in the centre will be in excess of 2m (6ft) high. *Eupatorium purpureum* 'Atropurpureum' in particular has impressive bulk as well as height, its dark pink flowers acting as a magnet for butterflies. Next to it, *Miscanthus sinensis* 'Malepartus' should begin to produce its reed-like flower stems at the same time and continue to look majestic through the winter, especially if it receives low winter sunlight. The other tall element is *Cimicifuga simplex* 'Pritchard's Giant', with long narrow spikes of white flowers above the impressively divided leaves.

Flower shapes provide some effective contrasts, for example the big, pink daisies of *Echinacea purpurea* 'Rubinglow' with the upright veronica behind it, and the yellow umbel shapes of *Achillea* 'Credo' to one side. Another good shape and colour combination comes from the lavender-blue wispy panicles of *Perovskia atriplicifolia* behind the solid, almost dumpy pink umbels of *Sedum* 'Matrona'. Many of the species have seed heads that provide extra winter attractions.

It is also worth noting that two of the plants are set very close together so that their shapes mingle. Both *Origanum* 'Rosenkuppel' and *Limonium latifolium* flower in mid- to late summer, the former having bunches of pink flowers and reddish bracts that continue to look good for many weeks after the flowers have died, and the latter a head of many tiny, lavender-coloured flowers. The origanum sends up occasional runners some distance from the parent plant, creating a rather attractive effect as new clusters appear scattered amongst other plants.

Besides the tall miscanthus, there are two shorter grasses. *Molinia caerulea* 'Moorhexe' grows 70cm (21/2ft) high with flowers and seed heads on tall stems that are initially vertical before arching outwards, and the slightly shorter *Schizachrium scoparium* 'The Blues' has blue-tinged foliage that turns pink or reddish in the autumn.

REQUIREMENTS

1. Full sun and an open site is needed for this scheme to flourish. Provide free-draining, fertile soil, but note that many species need ground that rarely dries out. The cimicifuga may be a problem in some areas because it needs cool conditions, the leaves reacting to heat or drought by turning brown. At high altitudes or latitudes it may be grown in sun, elsewhere it always flowers reliably, and in Piet's opinion the scorched leaves can easily be ignored. The achillea may be a problem because winter wet on some soils, eg. heavy clay ones, or where drainage is less than perfect, can cause the plant to rot.

2. The plants are mostly long-lived and cannot be expected to cause particular long-term management problems. The monarda may need replanting if its young shoots wander too far. the fennel may not survive the winter but will almost certainly self-sow around, and the phlox will need dividing and replanting after a number of years.

[Left] *Liatris spicata*

[Centre] *Veronicastrum virginicum* 'Fascination'

[Right] *Stachys monieri* 'Hummelo' with *Echinacea*

Gravel garden

plant list

1. *Dianthus amuriensis* (20)
2. *Stipa pulcherrima* (2)
3. *Acaena* 'Copper Carpet' (10)
4. *Thymus serpyllum* (4)
5. *Sedum* 'Fuldaglut' (12)
6. *Santolina pinnata* subsp. neapolitana 'Edward Bowles' (9)
7. *Stachys byzantina* 'Big Ears' (15)
8. *Eryngium bourgatii* (2)
9. *Sedum ruprechtii* (8)
10. *Geranium cinereum* 'Ballerina' (5)
11. *Stipa gigantea* (1)
12. *Ferula communis* (6)
13. *Euphorbia seguieriana* subsp. *niciciana* (6)
14. *Dictamnus albus* (6)
15. *Imperata cylindrica* (12)
16. *Tulipa hageri* 'Splendens' (30)
17. *Crocus sieberi* (100)
18. *Eryngium decaisneum* (2)

Ideal for a hot dry site, this planting aims at a scattered planting on gravel, with an emphasis on interesting evergreen foliage colours, a variety of textures and some dramatic shapes. Note how a limited palette of plants is used, and the way in which they are repeated, creating a natural rhythm.

Each drift will need a large batch of plants; you decide how many. If a fairly dense carpeting effect is wanted, plants can be set out at the distances suggested, but if a more sparse effect is sought with more gravel showing, use fewer plants. Note that some, notably the acaena, stachys and thyme, are strong spreaders.

The bushy, silver evergreen *Santolina pinnata* subsp. 'Edward Bowles' with creamy-white summer flowers and the low carpeting, silver-grey-leaved *Stachys* 'Big Ears' give winter interest, and contrast with the bronze-copper coloured *Acaena* 'Copper Carpet' (also called 'Kupferteppich'). Spring sees the pink-lilac *Crocus sieberi* and later scarlet *Tulipa hageri* 'Splendens' in flower.

In late spring and early summer, the flowering will be at its height. The carpets of *Thymus serpyllum* have pink flowers, *Geranium cinereum* 'Ballerina' has pink flowers intricately veined with a dark red-pink, and *Dianthus amuriensis* is mauve. In contrast, *Euphorbia seguieriana* subsp. *niciciana* forms mats of grey foliage covered with heads of greeny-yellow flowers for weeks on end.

The low, spiny-looking *Eryngium bourgatii* blooms a little later, its flowers being unusual, dark steel-blue over low grey foliage. *Stipa pulcherrima* also performs from early to midsummer, and is the most spectacular of all grasses with long awns, up to 60cm (2ft) long on each spikelet, that seem to float in the air, forever in motion. This magical effect only lasts a few weeks, after which the seeds blow away. *Stipa gigantea* looks good from early summer to late autumn, with its far-flung, oat-like panicles dangling from 1.5m (4ft) high stems. Though large, the plant is effectively transparent because it is easy to see through the stems. Another feature is *Dictamnus albus*, dotted around the planting with spikes of cream flowers. It produces so much volatile oil that on calm summer evenings you can put a match to it, causing a brief flair-up (with luck) which leaves the plant unscathed.

There is then little in flower until late summer or autumn, when the yellow *Sedum ruprechtii*, the carpeting, purple-leaved and red-flowering *Sedum* 'Fuldaglut' and the spectacular *Eryngium decaisneum* flower. The last thrusts out a 2–3m (6–10ft) flower spike topped by thimble-shaped, purple-brown heads. The other giant in the gravel bed is *Ferula communis*, that may take several years to build up a mound of dark feathery foliage, before producing a yellow flower head atop a 3m (10ft) high stem.

This scheme also includes some plants of the blood grass (*Imperata cylindrica*), whose deep red colour is spectacular when back-lit, making a striking contrast to the other plants here at the end of the year.

[Left] *Imperata cylindrica*

[Right] *Ferula communis*

REQUIREMENTS

1. This gravel bed is designed for an average, fertile but potentially dry site with free-draining (possibly stony or sandy) soil. Gravel should be chosen to complement the colour of the plants' foliage, and be applied after planting to a depth of around 3–5cm (1½–2in).

2. All the plants are reasonably long-lived although in nature the ferula is monocarpic (i.e. it dies after flowering). In cultivation this does not seem to happen, possibly because growing conditions are generally better in the garden. Long-term, beware the spreading tendencies of the thyme, stachys and acaena; if their growth is too exuberant and they start to smother other plants, their unwanted, offending growth can be easily pulled up.

3. The imperata is not reliably hardy in severe winters, but could be protected with a layer of straw or bracken weighed down with stones or bricks.

An early flowering border with good foliage

plant list

1. *Geranium phaeum* 'Album' (6)
2. *Hosta* 'Halcyon' (2)
3. *Astrantia major* 'Claret' (12)
4. *Luzula sylvatica* 'Wälder' (3)
5. *Geranium psilostemon* (5)
6. *Digitalis grandiflora* (10)
7. *Epimedium grandiflorum* (5)
8. *Geranium* × *oxonianum* 'Claridge Druce' (5)
9. *Cimicifuga simplex* 'Brunette' (4)
10. *Rodgersia* 'Die Anmutige' (2)
11. *Uvularia grandiflora* (2)
12. *Podophyllum hexandrum* 'Majus' (2)
13. *Carex muskingumensis* (1)
14. *Anemone rivularis* (3)
15. *Polystichum setiferum* 'Dahlem' (1)
16. *Hakonechloa macra* (1)
17. *Heuchera* 'Palace Purple' (3)
18. *Smilacina racemosa* (3)
19. *Geranium* 'Sirak' (5)

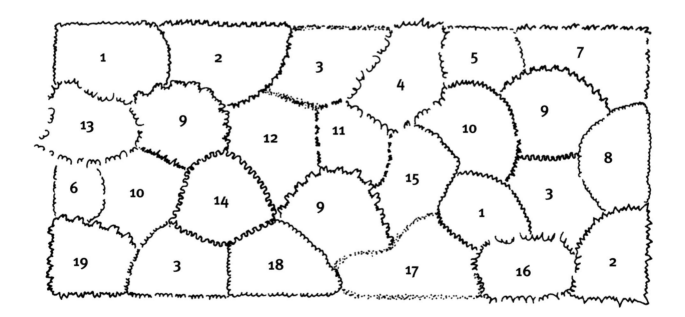

The plants in this scheme come from woodland-edge habitats, where they tend to flower early in the year but compensate by generally having good quality foliage. The best sites are under the outer canopy of a tree, on the shady side of a house, or on a slope facing away from the sun.

Late spring sees the pure white of *Geranium phaeum* 'Album', the lilac-pink of *Geranium* 'Sirak', white *Anemone rivularis*, and the dark red of *Astrantia major* 'Claret' among the fresh young growth of the fern *Polystichium setiferum* 'Dahlem', *Hosta* 'Halcyon', *Cimicifuga simplex* 'Brunette', *Podophyllym hexandrum* 'Majus' and *Rodgersia* 'Die Anmutige'.

Uvularia grandiflora is a woodland plant that also flowers around now, with elegant, yellow, bell-shaped flowers hanging from the upper part of upright 75cm (2½ft) high stems. The related *Smilacina racemosa* has upright stems, briefly complemented by a head of white flowers, and also has elegant foliage. *Digitalis grandiflora* sends up its spikes of large, pale yellow foxgloves somewhat later, while *Geranium* × *oxonianum* 'Claridge Druce' covers itself in deep pink flowers and the rodgersias produce their rather dramatic panicles, packed with thousands of tiny, creamy flowers.

The astrantia should flower several times through the season, and the *Geranium* × *oxonianum* 'Claridge Druce' will always flower again in late summer, and into the autumn if the ground has enough moisture. The start of the later part of the season features three plants of *Cimicifuga simplex* 'Brunette' with 2m (6ft) high stems carrying long, bending spikes of white flowers.

The joy of this planting lies in the variety of foliage shapes, with the main element being a contrast between large, bold leaves and finely divided ones. An additional element is the contrast between the various shades of green and the dark bronze-brown of the three cimicifugas, and the dark purple of *Heuchera* 'Palace Purple', the rodgersias and *Epimedium grandiflorum*.

The large-leaved plants include the hosta, rodgersia and the podophyllum. They contrast with the finely-divided polystichium fronds, the coarsely-divided leaves of the cimicifuga and the grassy linearity of the sedge (*Carex muskingumensis*) and the grass *Hakonechloa macra*. The former is a deep fresh green, and makes up for often being somewhat untidy by its healthy, vigorous look, and an unusual tufted growth pattern. The latter, however, always looks attractively neatly combed. *Luzula sylvatica* 'Wälder' is also linear in character, forming dense carpets of low tufted growth.

Only a couple of species here are evergreen, the luzula and polystichum, with the carex keeping its leaves until relatively late in mild climates.

Smilacina racemosa

REQUIREMENTS

1. The ideal site for this scheme receives a few hours of sun a day, or gets dappled sun beneath the outer canopy of deciduous trees. The soil should be free-draining without experiencing drought. Most of the plants will also flourish on soils that are definitely on the moist side, the hosta and rodgersia appreciating this particularly and being the first to suffer in dry conditions. Sites with tree roots that dry out the soil, or that are so close to buildings that rainfall is restricted, are not suitable unless irrigation is installed.

   The plants used that are most tolerant of dry shade include *Geranium phaeum*, the luzula and polystichum. The relative tolerance of the latter makes this a particularly useful fern.

2. An annual cutting down and removal of dead growth is the only regular maintenance needed. Several of the plants, the smilacina, podophyllum and uvularia particularly, also benefit from a humus-rich soil with plenty of organic matter. Composted plants could be applied as a winter mulch or, alternatively, they could be shredded and used as a mulch without composting.

3. The digitalis is the only short-lived or biennial species here, but on all soils, apart from very heavy ones, it will regenerate through self-sowing. *Geranium* × *oxonianum* 'Claridge Druce' is the only really potentially invasive species; it is a very strong grower and can seed itself around extensively. Cutting it back after flowering results in a tidier plant, and dividing it every few years will help keep it within bounds. The other species are long-lived and do not present any particular problems.

Nori and Sandra Pope

Since Nori and Sandra Pope took over the garden at Hadspen House, Somerset, UK, in 1987, it has become one of the most talked about gardens in Europe. The Popes' experimental colour plantings show a boldness and emotional depth that exceeds anything seen before.

The Canadian couple had seen the semi-derelict kitchen garden while on holiday and, hearing that it was up for rent, made the bold step of taking it on as a business, setting up a nursery and, within a few years, opening the garden to the public. 'Being Canadian,' emphasizes Nori, 'means that we don't come encumbered with so much history and are not hindered by so many boundaries.'

The area in which the Popes work at Hadspen was not designed for ornamental gardening, but they saw the neglected site as a 'romantic frame waiting for a painting'. The south-facing aspect suits an adventurous approach, and contains warm, sunny walls built in a D-shape, that originally would have sheltered peaches and early vegetables, and a terrace (the site of a long-demolished greenhouse) dramatically positioned above a large tank, that is now a lily pond bordered by lush, waterside plants.

The setting of hills and woodland seems to embrace the garden, which looks out over the mellow Somerset countryside. Shrubs planted by Penelope Hobhouse, who had lived there until 10 years before, provide the structure in parts of the garden, while a collection of hostas and other foliage perennials are a legacy of the late Eric Smith,

a plant breeder of legendary repute who Penelope took under her wing.

In his teenage years, Nori was as an apprentice gardener to an old Austrian nurseryman, in British Columbia, Canada, and learnt his gardening skills in a traditional setting before studying graphic arts. He returned to gardening professionally after his studies, and only thought about applying the lessons he had learnt at college when he met Sandra, who wanted to create a red garden. 'Sandra introduced me to colour, and when courting her I bought every red plant known to man.'

Creating the garden together is central to the Popes' achievement. The stereotypical gardening couple splits the work between the man who designs the framework and does the hard landscaping, and the woman who does the planting, but the Popes' gardening relationship is much more complex and subtle. Fundamental to their shared passion for colour is the knowledge that, on the whole, women can distinguish colours to a much finer degree than most men, and can remember them more accurately. Sandra's eye reigns supreme.

When talking to the Popes it is also clear that they are equally comfortable in different disciplines. 'We make no separation,' Nori says, 'between art, music and gardening.' And when discussing their approach to colour he and Sandra move from one subject to another with consummate ease, often using musical terms because 'gardening does not have its own language'. Sandra adds: 'If you take colour as the theme, then combinations of colour are the melody and we build on that thematically, arranging numbers of plants in ascending or descending order. It's the same way that someone composing a piece of music would build on, say, a chord to create a whole symphony.' She emphasizes that they don't 'just think about colour' but see it is a starting point. 'Colour is so diverse – you can make a monochrome border, or create one with harmonies and contrasts.'

It is the Popes' use of monochrome plantings that has created the biggest stir in the gardening community. They created a series of related monochrome themes in the long border against the semi-circular brick wall and a dramatic double yellow border with not only a wide variety of yellow

[left] A section of a red border at Hadspen House contains the annual *Zinnia peruviana* and *Crocosmia* 'Lucifer'

[Right] The famous yellow border

flowers, but also yellow-tinged and variegated foliage. Here, plants are grouped so that there are 'two tunes, related but distinct, twisted together visually'. They run through the yellow border, with clumps of ascending numbers of plants up the border on one side, with descending numbers in each clump on the other.

'A single-colour planting is essentially about harmony,' explains Nori, 'while mixed colours cancel each other out.' Freed from the task of having to see many different colours, the eye can then concentrate on appreciating other aspects of a planting, including the different flower shapes, and the subtle differences between the shades. However, recognizing that too much of one colour will saturate the eye, some relief is provided by a few blue flowers among the yellows.

They contrast their work with that of Christopher Lloyd whose garden at Great Dixter, East Sussex, UK, is very much about exploring contrasts, sometimes to the extent of deliberately provoking his visitors. For example he has juxtaposed orange and pink, a combination that most gardeners would shy away from. As a result Great Dixter is

a high energy garden, with little respite from visual stimulation, which Nori compares with modern dissonant composers such as Bartok. Colour changes at Hadspen are made more gradually and, with closely controlled tonal shifts and underlying melodies, are more akin to 19th-century symphonies.

'We use layers of music in the garden,' says Sandra, and when I ask about specific inspirations, Nori cites Mahler and Goretsky. On another occasion Nori says that he 'wanted to plant Mahler's 2nd Symphony'. He adds: 'You could give plants individual notes and then compose a border based on a piece of music; and then maybe plant another border and compose a musical piece based on your scheme.'

In painting, he lists Monet's use of rhythm, Rothko's use of colour, Bonnard's use of shadow and light, and 'any of the pointillists'. But whereas 'Monet and Renoir made gardens and interpreted them as paintings,' Sandra explains, 'we base gardens on paintings.' Nori adds that Monet's later work is a like a fabric, a mixture of colours. '
I find that inspirational,' he says.

Having explored single-colour plantings so thoroughly, the Popes are now moving on to different colour combinations. In order to maintain harmony, Nori suggests that combinations are made in 'half-tone jumps', for example using peach and yellow, or purple and blue. 'But if there is more than one combination,' he warns, 'it can become a jumble.'

Sandra adds that simply putting colours together does not get you very far. 'You have to look at what you can do with the plants,' she says. 'Do they, for example, provide the colour I want when I want? But plants selected for particular colour combinations should also be looked at within the context of the whole season. Do they have good winter stems, or berries, for example?' To some extent the limitations of a particular colour scheme may be overcome by intensive management, and Hadspen is no low-maintenance garden, as Sandra explains. 'We manipulate plants a lot, and cut them back when they have finished, and then plant out seasonal plants like argyranthemums and tulips.'

Tulips are indispensable for colour early in the season, as are dahlias later in the year. 'We have always loved tulips,' Nori explains, 'as do the mice,' adds Sandra. 'And we like single roses because so many old ones go so soggy in a wet English summer.' Few genera offer such a variety of colours as do the dahlias, many with a sumptuous, velvety depth. They are used in many different parts of the garden to concentrate the colour in a section of the themed border, and to extend its glory until the first frosts.

Annuals also enable the Popes to experiment with new schemes every year. They like to create rapid effects because they enjoy the fact that: 'Once it works that's also the end of it; gardening is an ephemeral process and next year you have to start again.' Vegetables are annuals too, and a vegetable area has long been a feature of the central part of the largest open space within the walled garden at Hadspen.

Concentrating on using varieties with coloured foliage, the Popes' vegetable garden is like no other, with purple kales, the glowing stems of ruby chard, dark-stemmed 'Sugar Dot' sweet corn and red-leaved lettuces. The Popes have even done some of their own plant selection with vegetables, producing the chard 'Hadspen Golden', whose broad golden-yellow stems glow in the low winter sun, and a cross between ruby chard and beetroot 'Bulls Blood', whose large leaves and stems are dark purple-red.

Nori has always been a bit of a plant collector, and this has been turned to good use in the couple's constant desire to, as he puts it, 'push the edge of what is possible' with colour. Working with the subtleties of colour requires a great deal of sifting through what is available and, as more plants come on the market, the range of possibilities increases. Of all the colours, the Popes are particularly fond of plum, the blend of red, blue and black.

Historically there has been a limited number of plum-coloured flowers, but recent plant selection has resulted in more, enabling the Popes to develop their most daring colour combinations. Plum with red foliage can be almost mournful, while green foliage highlights it and feels refreshing. Very dark plum shades combined with silver and grey foliage create a sense of drama and vibrancy. With orange, as in their plantings for this book, there is excitement with near-tropical lushness.

At their own home, near Hadspen, they are experimenting in a long thin border with 'plum, apricot, red, purple and blue, in a very wild style'. Their friend Piet Oudolf has dubbed it 'a meadow in a strip', using plants with lots of small leaves rather than dark or bold ones, so 'that the planting is sympathetic to the landscape'. The relationship with landscape is something that is beginning to occupy the Popes at Hadspen, too, as they look to its future development, aiming to simplify it and extend the garden into the landscape.

They are also on the lookout for new, large plants. 'Compact is not a word we want to hear,' says Nori. When I spoke to them they were very pleased with a recent acquisition, the seed of an enormous wild marigold they found in Kerala, India. 'There is a huge amount of exploration still to be done with colour,' Sandra adds, stressing again that 'new plants mean new combinations'.

Confident that they are just at the beginning, Nori and Sandra will no doubt carry on creating inspiring new plant combinations at Hadspen, agreeing very occasionally to design plantings for public places, for example a border at the Botanic Gardens, Oxford, UK, which is intended to be at its best in spring and autumn. They also act as consultants to a select number of garden designers and landscape architects, advising them on plant selection and combinations. The four plantings they have designed for this book, all based on a theme of orange and plum-purple, demonstrate their exciting use of colour.

Decorative vegetable garden in orange and plum

plant list

1. Lettuce 'Parella Red'	(20)	
2. Chard 'Hadspen Golden'	(20)	
3. Cabbage 'Red Jewel'	(8)	
4. Tomato 'Golden Sunrise'	(8)	
5. Beetroot 'Bull's Blood'	(30)	
6. Aubergine 'Bambino'	(8)	
7. Courgette 'Gold Rush'	(4)	
8. Kale 'Redbor'	(20)	
9. *Calendula officinalis*	(30)	
10. Basil 'Dark Opal'	(30)	
11. *Tagetes patula*	(30)	
12. Amaranthus 'Hopi Red'	(30)	
13. Sunflower 'Orange Sun'	(20)	
14. Zinnia 'Orange Cajun'	(30)	
15. Lettuce 'Bijou'	(20)	
16. *Tropaeolum majus* hybrid	(30)	
17. *Tropaeolum majus* Alaska Series	(2)	
18. Winter squash 'Kuri'	(2)	
19. Purple podded runner beans	(2)	
20. Sweet pea 'Beaujolais'	(2)	

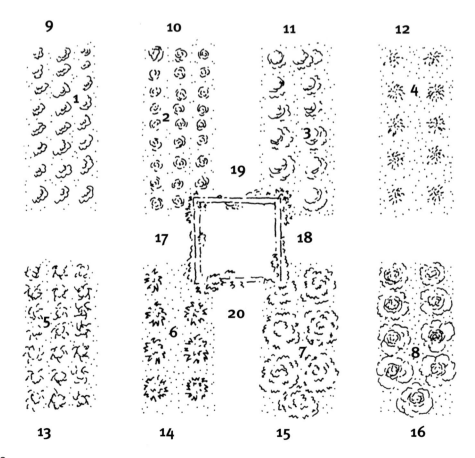

Gone are the days when vegetables were consigned to a part of the garden never to be viewed, except when digging or harvesting. Vegetables are now accepted as being beautiful in their own right, and varieties are being bred with coloured leaves or stems, or with fruit that is differently coloured to conventional varieties. This vibrant potager translates the Pope's theories about colour from the border to the vegetable garden, with vegetables and some flowers being laid out in beds, with a central pergola planted with flowers and vegetables.

The orange and plum colour scheme is effective with vegetables because so many have dark foliage – amaranthus, basil, beetroot, cabbage, kale and lettuce – while the runner bean has purple pods. The others here have orange flowers or fruit and, in the case of the courgette, yellow flowers and fruit. Chard 'Hadspen

Golden', one of several developed by the Popes, has orange stems and, like all chards, provides a nutritious spinach-like vegetable for almost 12 months of the year, both stems and leaves being edible. Amaranthus is a leaf vegetable that is eaten all over the tropics, and is a particular favourite in the Caribbean where it is known as 'callalloo'. Squash 'Kuri' is tangerine-orange while the sweet pea 'Beaujolais' has burgundy-red flowers.

The flowers are not just decorative. The English marigold (*Calendula officinalis*) can be eaten in salads, while the nasturtium (*Tropaeolum majus* hybrid) has hot tasting leaves that can be judiciously added to salads. Its seed pods can also be used in salads, and even pickled.

With a potager like this, the key to cultivation lies in the distinction between those vegetables and herbs that are

hardy and those that are half-hardy. Hardy kinds can be sown in the ground where they are to grow in spring, whereas half-hardy kinds need to be sown inside, in a greenhouse or on a light windowsill, well before they are planted out after the last frost. English marigold is a hardy annual, as is the beetroot, kale, chard and the two varieties of lettuce and nasturtium. The amaranthus and sunflower can be sown in late spring, but will make better growth if they are started off inside. All the others need a warm start inside, with the aubergine needing to be sown in early spring if it is to have any chance of producing fruit.

With all vegetables, particularly the half-hardy kinds, it is vital that the instructions on the packet are followed, and that they are sown at the times and temperatures recommended. The sweet pea has hard seed that germinates better if the seed coat is nicked with a knife, but ideally sow it in the autumn, and stand the pots out in a cold frame where they will survive the winter cold.

The vegetables can be harvested throughout the summer, with the lettuce being sown in succession to avoid any gaps, or leaves can be taken as and when required, without digging up the whole plant. It will be possible to harvest the chard throughout the winter if it is not too cold, while the kale will stand any amount of cold, making it one of the most useful winter vegetables.

REQUIREMENTS

1. Like all vegetables, these varieties benefit from plenty of sun, water and nutients. An open site that gets sun for most of the day is very important, as is fertile soil that never dries out. The soil should ideally be well-fed and supplied with plenty of organic matter: use well-rotted manure or garden compost in the autumn, and a general -purpose organic fertilizer before planting in the spring.

2. This is obviously a planting for one year only. If you like it so much that you want to repeat it next year or try a similar scheme, change the positions of the plants. Crop rotation is fundamental to good vegetable garden practice, and is discussed in detail in all books on vegetable gardening. Esentially it means you must not grow the same crop on the same patch of ground more than once in three years. It ensures that pests and diseases do not build up in the soil.

[Left] Courgette 'Gold Rush'

[Right] Kale 'Redbor'

[Left] *Miscanthus sinensis* 'Malepartus'

[Right] *Carex flagellifera*

[Below] *Dahlia* 'David Howard'

An autumn border in orange and plum

plant list

1. Heuchera 'Bressingham Bronze'	(12)
2. Dahlia 'David Howard'	(5)
3. Chrysanthemum 'Mary Stoker'	(3)
4. Amaranthus 'Hopi Red'	(20)
5. Cosmos sulphureus 'Sunset'	(12)
6. Miscanthus sinensis 'Malepartus'	(5)
7. Cosmos astrosanguineus	(6)
8. Helianthus 'Velvet Queen'	(7)
9. Rosa moyesii 'Geranium'	(1)
10. Dahlia 'Ellen Houston'	(5)
11. Helenium 'Chipperfield Orange'	(3)
12. Acer platanoides 'Crimson King'	(1)
13. Foeniculum vulgare 'Purpureum'	(7)
14. Buddleia × *weyeriana*	(1)
15. Helenium 'Moerheim Beauty'	(3)
16. Chrysanthemum 'Shelly'	(3)
17. Carex flagellifera	(5)
18. Atriplex hortensis var. *rubra*	(30)
19. Helianthus 'Floristan'	(7)

18 planted throughout

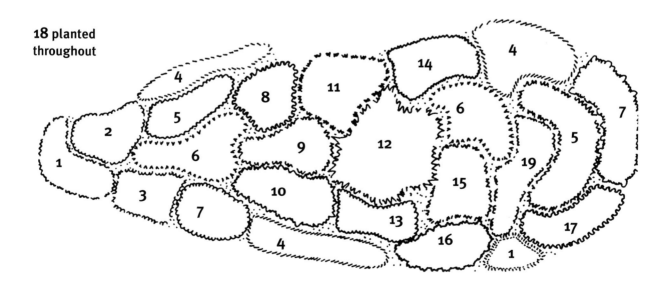

'Hot colours are prevalent at this time of year,' says Sandra. Certainly it does seem that there are more colours like red and orange in late summer and autumn, and this planting is designed to make the most of the various oranges using shrubs, perennials, grasses and annuals.

The centrepiece of the border is a maple (*Acer platanoides* 'Crimson King') that has deep crimson leaves, turning orange in autumn, and which is kept pollarded (ie. it has its branches cut back to the trunk every two years to keep it small). Next to it is *Buddleia × weyeriana* with panicles of pale orange flowers through summer, into the autumn. There is also a *Rosa moyesii* 'Geranium' that produces scarlet hips.

Apart from these woody plants, everything else in this border is a perennial or an annual, reflecting the fact that late-season colour primarily comes from non-woody plants. Members of the daisy family contribute some of the best colours in the orange part of the spectrum, especially at this time of year. They include *Chrysanthemum* 'Shelly' (deep copper) and *C*. 'Mary Stoker' (single, palest apricot), *Helenium* 'Moerheim Beauty' (rich browny-red) and *H*. 'Chipperfield Orange' – all are hardy perennials, and can be regarded as permanent parts of the planting.

The dahlias include 'David Howard' (amber-orange) and 'Ellen Houston' (orange), both of which are half-hardy, needing lifting and protecting under cover over winter. There are two sunflowers, *Helianthus* 'Floristan' (red-orange) and *H*. 'Velvet Queen' (dark burgundy-brown),

and *Cosmos sulphureus* 'Sunset' (amber-orange), all of which are annuals. The predominately orange tones of the flowers are balanced by the purple and plum-tinged foliage of the maple, by *Amaranthus* 'Hopi Red', the bronze fennel (*Foeniculum vulgare* 'Purpureum'), *Atriplex hortensis* var. *rubra* and *Heuchera* 'Bressingham Bronze'.

The effect of the striking colours is enhanced by interesting textural elements. Look at the tight red flower and seed heads of the amaranthus, the rosettes of the fine brown grass, the foliage of *Carex flagellifera* and the very dark, light-absorbing matt foliage of the fennel. The stately grass *Miscanthus sinensis* 'Malepartus' has red-tinged flower panicles, while its more subtle shades and grassy texture add a calming note to these strong colours.

Scent plays its part too, with *Cosmos atrosanguineus* providing mysterious dark red flowers and the most delicious scent of chocolate, an endless source of interest and amusement.

[Left] *Cosmos atrosanguineus*

[Right] A border designed by the Popes in the Oxford Botanic Garden in early autumn with blazing *Dahlia* 'David Howard' and *Helenium* 'Chipperfield Orange'

REQUIREMENTS

1. Any site which receives full sun on a reasonably fertile, moisture-retentive soil will support these plants.

2. This combination includes permanent woody and herbaceous plants, and seasonal plants. The dahlias need protecting over winter, as will the *Cosmos atrosanguineus* in cold winter gardens, while the amaranthus and atriplex are hardy annuals, and the *Cosmos sulphureus* is a half-hardy annual (sow its seed under cover in spring). The atriplex and amaranthus can usually be guaranteed to self-seed, and will reappear every year scattered throughout the border. Both can be used as a spinach-like leaf vegetable.

3. The perennial elements will ensure a good long-term result, although the buddleia will grow large and may need ruthless pruning, even annual cutting back to the ground, if required, to stop it becoming too big.

A damp border in orange and plum

plant list

1. Tropaeolum speciosum	(3)
2. Corylus maxima 'Purpurea'	(1)
3. Rhododendron 'Brazil'	(1)
4. Veratrum nigrum	(5)
5. Canna 'Lesotho Lill'	(5)
6. Ligularia dentata 'Desdemona'	(5)
7. Euphorbia griffithii 'Fireglow'	(5)
8. Lilium henryi	(12)
9. Phormium tenax	(5)
10. Angelica gigas	(9)
11. Trollius chinensis 'Golden Queen'	(5)
12. Primula bulleyana	(15)
13. Meconopsis cambrica	(30)
14. Plantago major 'Rubrifolia'	(10)
15. Mimulus cardinalis	(10)
16. Epimedium × warleyense	(10)
17. Geum 'Georgenberg'	(10)
18. Hemerocallis fulva	(4)

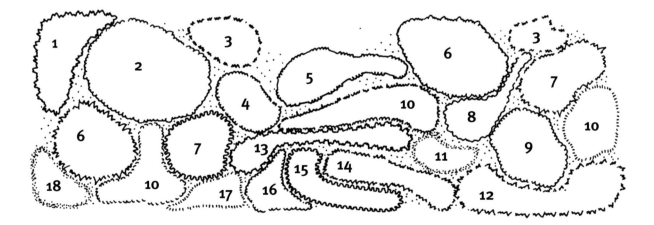

'People usually think of green as being the predominant colour in damp places, says Sandra, 'and this combination of orange and plum is not often seen. It's an opportunity to make a hot and lush border.

The planting brings together striking plant forms, often characteristic of species that thrive in moist habitats, and a dramatic colour combination of hot colours and purples. The border's evergreen lynchpin is *Phormium tenax*, with its copper-coloured, sword-like leaves. During the growing season a number of herbaceous species with bold foliage complement it. They include *Veratrum nigrum,* with its unusual, pleated leaves, the orange *Canna* 'Lesotho Lill', with broad, tropical-looking foliage and *Angelica gigas*, a biennial cow-parsley relative with dark purple flowers, plum-tinged foliage and an architectural form.

The purple-leaved hazel (*Corylus maxima* 'Purpurea') exerts a powerful influence on the border throughout the summer, although the fiery appearance of the azalea (*Rhododendron* 'Brazil') will act as a dramatic contrast during early summer when it is flowering. The dark foliage theme is carried further by *Ligularia dentata* 'Desdemona',

with its large mahogany leaves and orange flowers, and the plantain (*Plantago major* 'Rubrifolia').

The orange theme starts in spring with the delicate flowers of *Epimedium* × *warleyense*, whose fresh green leaves add a light touch among so much dark foliage. It extends into late spring with *Trollius chinensis* 'Golden Queen', the short-lived and often self-seeding *Meconopsis cambrica* and the delightful, soft orange *Geum* 'Georgenburg'.

Euphorbia griffithii 'Fireglow' is a darker, almost red colour, while *Hemerocallis fulva* is a yellow, with a much more elegant appearance than most of the day lilies. Early to midsummer sees the dull orange turk's cap flowers of that tallest of lilies, *Lilium henryi*, the orange-red of *Mimulus cardinalis* creeping along at the front, and the warm tones of *Primula bulleyana*, one of the candelabra species, so-called because the flowers appear in whorls up the stems. The clump of cannas provides a strong central stand of orange for mid- to late summer, and the season ends with the spectacular scarlet of *Tropaeolum speciosum* climbing over the purple hazel.

[Left] *Crocosmia*
'Star of the East' with *Carex flagellifera*

[Right] *Angelica gigas*

REQUIREMENTS

1. Most of the plants need soil that is moist but definitely not waterlogged, although the ligularia copes well in very wet soil. The azalea and the tropaeoleum need acid soil. Light shade probably offers the most suitable conditions for the majority of plants, but if the soil never dries out they should flourish in full sun.

2. *Angelica gigas* is biennial, and seed should be sown annually for flowering the following year. The canna is not hardy; in mild climates it may be protected over winter by an insulating layer of straw, but in colder areas it is better to lift the tubers and store them in a frost-free place inside.

3. Most of the plants are long-lived and, eventually, some will form extensive patches. The epimedium and geum make useful ground-cover, but the *Euphorbia griffithii* might eventually take up too much space and need thinning out. Others are less long-lived, but have the capacity to self-sow and regenerate themselves.

The meconopsis and mimulus survive for only a few years but they self-sow well (occasionally to nuisance proportions), while the primula builds into clumps and self-sows. The end result may well be an exuberant mass of new plants. Rarely, however, will all spread equally well, and in time one will predominate, possibly at the expense of others. So be ready with the hoe to thin out any excess seedlings of the more dominant species.

Dry gravel bed in orange and plum

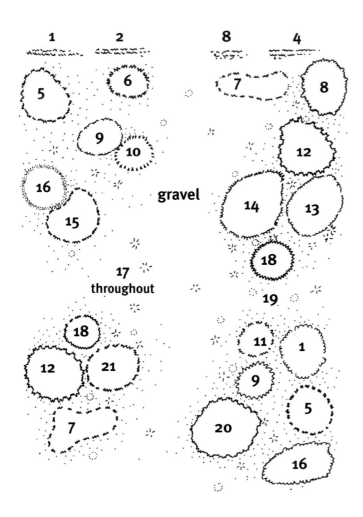

plant list

1. *Vitis vinifera* 'Purpurea' (1)
2. *Ipomoea lobata* (2)
3. *Clematis viticella* 'Purpurea Plena Elegans' (2)
4. *Rosa* 'Ghislaine de Féligonde' (1)
5. *Colutea* × *media* (2)
6. *Dahlia* 'Ellen Houston' (3)
7. *Achillea* 'Terracotta' (10)
8. *Salvia officinalis* 'Purpurascens' (5)
9. *Verbascum* 'Cotswold Queen' (6)
10. *Arctotis* × *hybrida* 'Flame' (30)
11. *Foeniculum vulgare* 'Purpureum' (6)
12. *Kniphofia caulescens* (3)
13. *Berberis* × *ottawensis* 'Superba' (1)
14. *Tropaeolum majus* 'Hermine Grashoff' (7)
15. *Leonotis nepetifolia* (7)
16. *Cotinus* 'Grace' (1)
17. *Eschscholzia californica* (50)
18. *Tithonia rotundifolia* 'Torch' (7)
19. *Allium atropurpureum* (50)
20. *Sedum telephium* subsp. *maximum* 'Atropurpureum' (8)
21. *Crocosmia* 'Star of the East' (10)

Ipomoea lobata

'I envisage this planting scheme as a garden behind a terraced house,' says Nori. 'It is a narrow strip that uses the whole width of a sunny garden, with honey-coloured matt gravel instead of soil, and creates the impression of being dry.' The gravel is also a wonderful foil for almost any colour, and reduces maintenance through dramatically reducing the ability of weed seeds to germinate in it.

Plants with strongly coloured flowers and/or leaves set amongst gravel create a strong tropical look, enhanced by climbers on the sunny wall behind. The purple-leaved vine (*Vitis vinifera* 'Purpurea') is echoed by the foliage tones of *Cotinus* 'Grace', *Berberis* × *ottawensis* 'Superba', the evergreen *Salvia officinalis* 'Purpurascens', the herbaceous purple fennel (*Foeniculum vulgare* 'Purpureum') and *Sedum maximum* 'Atropurpureum'.

These purple foliage tones are up picked by the maroon-purple flowers of *Clematis viticella* 'Purpurea Plena Elegans' borne in mid- to late summer, and the dark violet-mauve globes of the ornamental onion (*Allium atropurpureum*), scattered throughout the planting. Contrasting with these plummy tones are variations on orange and subtle reds. On the wall is the climbing rose 'Ghislaine de Féligonde', with orange-yellow flowers, and the half-hardy climber *Ipomoea lobata*, with distinctive flowers in one-sided clusters, the dark red flowers fading through orange to cream as they age. A similar effect is found with *Kniphofia caulescens*, whose massive clumps

of linear grey leaves produce dark red flower spikes in late summer, at about the same time as the ipomoea, fading in similar fashion to cream. *Achillea* 'Terracotta' has red flowers that fade to a paler, duller colour in early to midsummer. They are followed by the late summer, bright orange flowers of *Leonotis nepetifolia*, *Dahlia* 'Ellen Houston', the annual *Tithonia rotundifolia* 'Torch' and the double nasturtium *Tropaeolum* 'Hermione Grasshoff', while *Arctotis* × *hybrida* 'Flame' has terracotta flowers that fade to orange.

More subtle flower tones include the shrub *Colutea* × *media*, with pea-like blooms in a delicate shade of copper-bronze set against a sage-green filigree leaf in midsummer, and *Crocosmia* 'Star of the East', whose flowers are apricot-yellow. The crocosmia is one of the boldest of its kind, with sword-like leaves that contrast with the more rounded shapes of the rest of the plants. Most subtle of all is *Verbascum* 'Cotswold Queen', with flowers in a soft shade of orange-buff – a colour that stands out all the more for being surrounded by strongly coloured neighbours.

Scattered throughout is the annual California poppy (*Eschscholzia californica*), whose flowers come in a variety of shades of orange, yellow and cream. They self-seed throughout the gravel every year, as do those of the fennel, the verbascum and, in some gardens, the allium. Self-sowing is always difficult to predict, however.

[Below] *Crocosmia* 'Star of the East'

REQUIREMENTS

1. This scheme is for a sunny site because the strong colours look best in good light, and because many of the species used are from relatively warm climates. The planting is a mix of reliably hardy, long-lived species, one-season annuals and tender perennials that need protecting over winter. This means that the colour scheme has a solid, permanent framework, including varieties with purple foliage, such as the cotinus and the fennel, for the background, and elements that can be changed every year. An annual exercise in creativity is the result, when you must decide what works well with the framework plants.

2. The dahlia is half-hardy, and needs to be lifted after the first frost and stored in a frost-free place, and the arctotis needs lifting and looking after in a conservatory, or you can take cuttings in late summer and overwinter them inside. The mina and the tithonia are also half-hardy but are normally treated as annuals, being raised from seed indoors in spring, and planted out after the last frost. The eschscholzia is a hardy annual and will often self-sow itself, and in mild winters even survives for a second year. Although the achillea is totally hardy, it will not survive mild wet winters, damp being the major problem.

3. Gravel is a key part of this composition, but it needs to be in a colour that will complement the plants' flower and leaf colours; for example, soft yellow gravel will work much better than grey. It is normally applied after planting, filling the gaps between the plants to a depth of 3–5cm (1½–2in). If any planting is carried out after the gravel has been applied, care must be taken to avoid mixing the soil and gravel. Once appreciable quantities of soil get mixed in, there is a greater likelihood of unwanted weeds getting established.

[Above Left] *Cotinus* 'Grace'

[Above Right] *Kniphofia caulescens*

Index

Acknowledgements

Cassell Illustrated would like to thank the following photographers for permission to reproduce their pictures:

Mark Bolton (4, 9, 16, 18, 19, 25, 26–27, 28, 29, 36–37, 39, 40–41, 43, 45, 46–47, 49 (middle and bottom), 51 (bottom), 55, 59, 60, 61, 67, 68, 69, 70, 71, 76, 77, 84, 92, 94–95, 96, 103 (left), 104, 105, 107, 109 (top left), 110, 113, 115, 120–121, 127, 132, 136, 137, 140–141, 145 (top), 148 (right), 151, 152 (right), 155 (right), 157, 163, 164, 166, 169 (left), 173, 174, 175, 178, 179, 182, 183, 184–185); John Brookes (49 (top)); Garden Picture Library: (51 (top left, John Glover), 52 (Howard Rice), 65 (right, Juliette Wade), 75 (Howard Rice), 79 (Jacqui Hurst), 85 (Jerry Pavia) 87 (left Neil Holmes, right David Russell), 88 (Brian Carter), 99 (left J. S. Sira, right Howard Rice), 101 (John Glover), 109 (top right Jerry Pavia, bottom J. S. Sira), 123 (Georgia Glynn-Smith), 124 (John Glover), 125 (Neil Holmes), 129 (left Jo Whitworth, right Howard Rice), 131 (top Brian Carter, bottom right John Glover), 135 (Howard Rice), 147 (Howard Rice), 148 (left Chris Burrows), 152 (left Roger Hyam), 155 (left Sunniva Harte), 156 (Howard Rice), 169 (right Emma Peios), 170 (Mayer/Le Scanff), 171 (Clive Nicholls), 181 (Sunniva Harte)); Harpur Garden Library (14, 51 (top left), 56, 63, 64, 65 (left), 72, 80, 81, 83, 89, 91, 93, 103 (right), 149, 153, 159, 160, 177); Noël Kingsbury (11, 116, 117, 118); Andrew Lawson (32, 44, 139, 145 (bottom)); Marianne Majerus (13, 20, 23, 35, 119, 131 (bottom left), 165); Clive Nicholls (6, 8, 142, 143)